DATE DUE

MAR 1 9 1996			
APR 0 3 1996			
MAR 1 8 1997			
MAY 0 5 1997			
3-8-99			
MAR 23 1999			
GAYLORD			PRINTED IN U.S.A.

The *Peace* COMMANDOS

NONVIOLENT HEROES IN THE STRUGGLE AGAINST WAR AND INJUSTICE

Michael Kronenwetter

A TIMESTOP BOOK

New Discovery Books
New York

Maxwell Macmillan Canada
Toronto

Maxwell Macmillan International
New York Oxford Singapore Sydney

Design: Deborah Fillion

New Discovery Books
Macmillan Publishing Company
866 Third Avenue
New York, NY 10022

Maxwell Macmillan Canada, Inc.
1200 Eglinton Avenue East
Suite 200
Don Mills, Ontario M3C 3N1

Macmillan Publishing Company is part of the Maxwell Communication Group of Companies.

First Edition

Printed in the United States of America

10 9 8 7 6 5 4 3 2 1

Library of Congress Cataloging-in-Publication Data
Kronenwetter, Michael.
    The peace commandos : nonviolent heroes in the struggle against war and injustice / by Michael Kronenwetter. — 1st ed.
        p.   cm.
    Includes bibliographical references and index.
    ISBN 0-02-751051-4
    1. Peace movements—United States—History. 2. Vietnamese Conflict, 1961–1975—Protest movements—United States. I. Title.
JX1961.U6K76   1994
327.1'72'0973—dc20   93-31204
    Summary: A history of peace movements in the United States, including discussions of the principles behind nonviolent resistance and civil disobedience.

Contents

Preface

The United States has been involved in many wars—big and small, declared and not declared—and it has won most of them. Today, it is by far the most powerful military nation on earth. Most Americans are proud of these facts. They do not desire war, but they accept it as a necessary evil in a dangerous world.

There has always been, however, a minority of Americans who refuse to believe that war is necessary. Pacifists and others, who oppose specific wars on principle, have protested against American involvement in every war that the country has fought. They have spoken out even when they were called cowards and traitors for doing so. They have demonstrated in the streets, refused to serve in the military, and sometimes gone to jail rather than participate in wars in which they did not believe. They became, in effect, commandos in a nonviolent war against war itself.

This book is not a complete history of the American peace movement. It is an introduction. In it, you will meet the members of this brave and often misunderstood minority and the ideas that drive them. These are controversial people, and even more controversial ideas. You may find them appealing or outrageous. But they will challenge you, as they have challenged governments and armies around the world.

Allison Krause

Kent State University, Ohio — May 4, 1970

T housands of students gathered in the sunny commons area of the Kent State University campus that Monday afternoon. About a thousand of them, there to protest against U.S. involvement in the war in Vietnam, massed below the knoll near Taylor Hall. The others stood around the edges of the commons, watching with varying degrees of curiosity, excitement—and nervousness.

The demonstrators weren't supposed to be there. The authorities had banned campus rallies since the previous Saturday night, when a handful of radical students had fire-bombed the ROTC building. Ohio's governor, James Rhodes, had called the National Guard to the school to keep things quiet. They had been on campus since Sunday, and they were there now, eyeing the students warily from their formation near the remains of the ROTC building not far away. Even in the warm May sunshine, the guardsmen made a chilling sight in their battle uniforms, complete with helmets and gas masks and carrying their deadly looking M-1 rifles.

Guard or no guard, many students had come there determined to defy the ban. Hundreds of others—many of them equally opposed to the war—stumbled upon the demonstration by accident on their way to or from class. Some saw the guardsmen with their weapons and hurried on. Some joined the onlookers. Others joined the protestors.

Allison Krause was one of them.

Allison and her boyfriend, Barry, had come upon the demonstration as they walked across campus. They joined the crowd as protestors and guardsmen eyed each other warily across the grassy commons. The two groups were close in age, and many were close in background, too. Some of the guardsmen had signed up to avoid being drafted and sent to Vietnam. Some of the protesting students had considered signing up themselves, for the same reason.

But, despite the similarities, there was a tense hostility between them. For many of the protestors, the uniformed guardsmen symbolized the war they hated. For many of the guardsmen, the students were spoiled, unpatriotic brats.

Besides, the authorities had ordered the students to disperse, and the students weren't budging. Neither group knew for sure what the other would do next.

Despite the tensions that crackled over the commons like an electric charge, the students thought it was important to stay where they were. They wanted to show that they were not afraid. This was *their* campus, not the governor's. Certainly not the guards'. And they wanted to make a statement: a statement in favor of peace and against the war in Vietnam.

Different students were protesting the war for different reasons. Some feared being drafted and being sent to fight. Some hated the war because they had lost a friend or family member. Some believed in leftist revolution, and thought the United States was on the wrong side in the conflict. Still others hated the war simply because they believed in peace.

Allison Krause was one of them.

Although she was only 19 years old, Allison had already proved herself to be the kind of young woman who cared deeply about other people, and about making the world a better place to be. Even in high school, she had set aside time to help a retarded child and serve as a volunteer in a local hospital. Allison was distressed by the violence that had broken out on the Kent State campus. She had been particularly upset by the destruction of the ROTC building. But she was even more upset by the war in Vietnam, and by the arrival of armed troops on her campus. It was as though the war had come to Kent State.

Characteristically, Allison had met the growing tensions with a small gesture of gentleness and peace. The day before, she had walked up to one of the National Guardsmen and gently set a flower in the barrel mouth of his M-1. "Flowers are better than bullets,"[1] she had told him. Now, only a day later, some of the guardsmen's rifles were raised and pointing toward Allison and the other students.

Unlike the protest on Saturday night, however, this demonstration was peaceful. The armed presence of the guard was troubling, but the students were nonviolent. This was the kind of demonstration Allison could join.

But then the nature of the event began to change. A pair of National Guard jeeps swept out across the grass. Officers in the jeeps shouted through bullhorns, ordering the students to leave. They were met with jeers and insults, but the guard had decided to break up the demonstration. Acting on orders, several of the guardsmen fired tear gas canisters toward the demonstrators. Gas masks in place and marching in rough formation, line behind menacing line, the guardsmen began advancing on the students.

The young people retreated, but a few stopped to pick up fuming canisters and throw them back toward the troops. Others threw stones or bottles. The guardsmen paused briefly to fire new volleys of gas, then advanced on the students again, driving them over the knoll and down toward a large parking lot. The process continued until the guardsmen ran out of tear gas canisters. Then, as though frightened, they began hurrying back the way they came.

Seeing the guardsmen retreat, one group of students turned and followed, taunting the retreating soldiers. Some threw more rocks and pieces of broken concrete at the guardsmen. Few, if any, of those missiles hit their targets.

Allison opposed violence of any kind. She hated the war and felt bound to protest against it, but not with violence. She and Barry decided it was time to go. They began walking away. Behind them, some of the guardsmen had already stopped and wheeled toward the mocking students. Now they raised their rifles into firing position. They had raised them before, without firing, to frighten the students and keep them at bay.

But this time would be different.

This time, a barrage of shots rang out.

The shooting lasted only two or three seconds at the most, but an incredible number of shots were fired in that brief time. When it was over, 14 students lay bleeding on the ground. One young man was paralyzed from the waist down. Four other students were dead.

Allison Krause was one of them.

Chapter One

Warriors *for* Peace

E verybody wants peace. Nobody wants war. At least that's what they say.

Statesmen, members of the clergy, ordinary citizens—even military leaders—all proclaim their hatred of war. War is "all hell," declared the Civil War general William Tecumseh Sherman. "No one who has been to a war ever wants to see another one,"[1] insisted Marine Col. Oliver North, who served in Vietnam before working in President Reagan's White House. And yet, General Sherman was infamous for laying waste to Georgia in his "march to the sea," and Colonel North was caught secretly and illegally supplying U.S. arms to rebel forces in Central America.

Warfare has been a blight on human history for as long as history has been written. In fact, written history began as little more than a chronicle of wars. And there has been more warfare in the 20th century than ever before. Two massive world wars were followed by a so-called cold war that threatened the world with nuclear annihilation for 50 years, while hundreds of smaller "hot wars" continued to break out all over the globe. In 1993, roughly 40 military conflicts were raging in various places around the world.[2]

We Americans like to think of ourselves as an especially peace-loving people. Yet, in the two short centuries of our nation's history, U.S. military forces have been involved in more than 200 conflicts around the world. That adds up to approximately one for each year of the nation's existence—not counting the American Revolution, the Civil War, and the Indian wars, which took place on our own territory![3]

No matter how much lip service most Americans give to peace, they usually end up supporting U.S. war efforts, at least at first. Serious doubts sometimes surface later, but when the weapons of war are first rolled out, most Americans can be found cheering from the sidelines.

What is true of us is true of citizens of other nations as well. They disapprove of war in general, but they make an exception for those wars their government decides to fight. Most people would consider it unpatriotic—maybe even treasonous—not to support their country's war effort. Most. But not all. There have always been some thoughtful people who refused to answer their government's call to war.

These are people who do more than oppose war in silence. They act on their beliefs. They object. They protest. They take a stand. While their fellow citizens sign up to become soldiers in their country's wars, they enlist in another kind of fight. They become, in effect, commandos for peace: combatants in a war against war itself. While ordinary warriors fight with guns and bombs and missiles, these peaceful warriors fight with ideas, with words, and with nonviolent protest.

They have usually been a minority, and often a tiny minority. But they have had a power and influence far beyond their numbers. Often belittled as harmless eccentrics, or attacked as dangerous crackpots, the peace commandos have sometimes touched the conscience of the world. At times—as in India in the first half of the 20th century and in the United States in the 1960s—they have helped create social movements and to change the course of whole societies.

17

Who the Peace Commandos Are

Peace commandos come from all walks of life. They are students, teachers, lawyers, laborers, philosophers, politicians, housewives, writers, and scientists, past and present. Their ranks include anyone who has taken a moral stand against organized violence, and who has acted on that stand. Many famous people have been peace commandos, including:

Muhammad Ali—heavyweight champion boxer

Clarence Darrow—lawyer

Albert Einstein—scientist

Henry Ford—industrialist, founder of Ford Motor Company

Rev. Martin Luther King, Jr.—minister and activist

John Lennon—singer and songwriter

Linus Pauling—Nobel Prize-winning scientist

Dr. Benjamin Spock—pediatrician

Henry David Thoreau—author and naturalist

Count Leo Tolstoy—author

But most peace commandos are not famous. They are as anonymous and unknown as Allison Krause would have been, had she not fallen victim to an equally anonymous guardsman's bullet.

The peace commandos fight their nonviolent battle

against war in many ways. Some, like Thoreau and Tolstoy, fight with words. Some simply refuse to participate in what they believe to be the madness and injustice of war. Others fight through the political system. Still others, like the students at Kent State, demonstrate in the streets or on college campuses. Some go to jail for their beliefs. Some go into exile. Some of the very bravest put their bodies in the way of the weapons of war, sacrificing their own lives to save the lives of others.

A Personal Decision

Peace commandos are just like the rest of us in most ways, but they are different in one very special way: They take personal responsibility for decisions of war and peace.

Most people leave such decisions to their political leaders. Whatever their personal opinions and feelings, they accept the government's authority to tell them when to go to war. Peace commandos do not. They look to a higher authority than the government to make such momentous decisions. For some of them, that authority is religious. For others, it is their own conscience. But, for all of them, it is a choice they must make themselves.

Government officials make decisions of war and peace on the basis of the "national interest." They define that interest in political, economic, and military terms. Will going to war improve the United States' position in the world? Will it make the nation more secure? Will it promote trade and stimulate the economy? Will it strengthen America's military alliances?

Peace commandos, on the other hand, tend to think in human and moral terms. Is the war to be fought for a good cause? How many people will be killed? Maimed? Made homeless? Considering the devastation and misery, is this war justified? Can any war *ever* be justified?

Not all peace commandos think alike, of course. Some oppose only particular wars that they consider to be unjust. Others are absolute pacifists who oppose *all* wars, no matter how good the cause. Some go even further. They oppose violence of any kind, even when used in self-defense.

The Religious Pacifists

Several of the world's great spiritual leaders have rejected violence, often in very similar words. Consider the almost identical instructions of Siddhartha Gautama, who is known as the

Buddha, and Jesus Christ. "Overcome anger with love," advised the Buddha. "Shame on him that strikes; greater shame on him who stricken, strikes back."[4] "But I say to you not to resist the evildoer," commanded Jesus. "If someone strike thee on the right cheek, turn to him the other also."[5]

Jesus had other things to say about violence as well, even violence in the most noble of causes. When a disciple drew a weapon to fend off enemies attempting to seize Jesus, the founder of Christianity ordered him to "put back thy sword into its place, for all those who take the sword will perish by the sword."[6] "Blessed are the peacemakers,"[7] proclaimed Jesus on another occasion, and in fact, the early Christians were pacifists.[8] There is no evidence of Christians serving in the military until A.D. 170, and even after that, many Christians considered war incompatible with their religious beliefs.[9] This changed in the 4th century, when the Roman emperor Constantine I converted to Christianity and proceeded to conquer much of the known world in the name of Christ.

Today, only a handful of religious denominations (Christian or otherwise) preach pacifism. Even fewer teach that all violence is wrong. The Quaker (or Society of Friends), Mennonite, and Brethren churches are among the handful of Christian pacifist denominations. They believe that Christ's command not to resist the evildoer forbids them to partici-

21

pate in any kind of violence. Jehovah's Witnesses refuse to serve in the military because they will not give allegiance to any government. Sufism, a mystic branch of the Islamic faith, teaches that evil cannot be overcome by violence, but only with tolerance and love.

But most religions stop short of condemning war and violence altogether. Some often do just the opposite, actually urging their members to go to war. During the Middle Ages, Christian popes launched a series of military Crusades to wrest the Holy Land from the Muslims. Certain Islamic leaders have called for jihad, or "holy war," against those they see as the enemies of Islam. Jihad does not necessarily mean armed conflict. It can also refer to a political or ideological struggle. But it can, and as used by certain Islamic leaders sometimes does, mean full-scale military warfare

Ministers, priests, rabbis, and other clergy members usually reflect the political beliefs of the societies they live in. Once a nation is primed for war, the members of the clergy tend to get swept along by the same passions that drive other citizens. Many serve as chaplains, giving the combatants comfort and encouragement to carry on the fight. Some have literally blessed warships, fighter planes, and other weapons of war, asking God to give them success in destroying the enemy.

Not all religious pacifists belong to the so-called peace churches like the Mennonites or Quakers. Some Catholics and Jews, for example, believe that the scriptures condemn war, even though many authorities in their religions disagree.

Humanitarian Pacifists

Not all peace commandos are religious. Some are atheists, who have no particular religious beliefs at all. The Nobel Prize-winning mathematician and philosopher Bertrand Russell was one famous example.

Most nonreligious pacifists reject war for humanitarian reasons. They believe that human life should be valued for its own sake and that war denies that value. War is an attempt to solve problems by force of arms, and those who favor it assume that solving the problem is more important than the lives of the people who will be killed.

War has always involved killing. Modern methods of warfare involve the killing of many more people than ever before. And—given the nature of modern bombs, missiles, and other 20th-century weapons—the deaths inevitably include large numbers of children and other civilians. More than 37 million people were killed or wounded in World War I. Only a generation later, World War II killed more than 55 million and wounded at least 100 million more. The great majority of the people who died in World War I—roughly 30 million defenseless children, women, and noncombatant men—were civilians.[10]

Nonreligious pacifists reject the idea that such horrors can ever be justified for humanist reasons. What problem can be so unbearable that solving it is worth the deaths and mutilations of a hundred million people? For these pacifists, the idea that *any* problem can be solved by killing someone seems foolish. The idea that some wrongs, however terrible they may be, can be corrected by mass slaughter seems insane.

The idea of war in the nuclear age, say the humanitarian pacifists, is even more insane than the idea of war in the past. Today's sophisticated weapons can destroy not only whole cities, but whole nations. Some scientists believe nuclear weapons could actually wipe out all human life. With this possibility hanging over the world, pacifists of all kinds insist that rational people must find better ways to solve their conflicts than by using force.

The Theory of a "Just War"

How do people who are not total pacifists decide which wars are justified and which are not? Most use some version of a "just war" theory, a set of conditions by which to judge whether going to war is justified in a particular case.

One of the first just war theories in the Western world was proposed by the Christian philosopher St. Augustine in the 4th century. The Christian community was in the process of abandoning the pacifism it had preached since the time of Christ. Nonetheless, the early Christians recognized that war was still a terrible evil. They felt the need for a moral standard to apply in deciding when to risk that great evil in the service of an even greater good.

The 13th-century Italian philosopher and theologian St. Thomas Aquinas proposed what is probably the best-known of all just war theories, and there have been many others since. There are some important variations among them. Most of the early just war theories insist that a just war must be declared by a legitimate government, for example. But some modern just war theories reject this condition because it rules out any kind of revolutionary wars, even against the most cruel and tyrannical governments. But most just war theories, past and present, agree on at least four conditions for a just war:

1. The war must be fought for a good reason. No war can be considered just if it is fought for a trivial or immoral reason. Frivolous reasons might include avenging a diplomatic insult or settling a minor border dispute. Immoral reasons would include ethnic or religious hatred or the desire to conquer another nation's territory.

In order to be just, the goal for which the war is fought must be obtainable. The enormous devastation of war can only be justified—if ever—when it is likely to accomplish a real good. No war should ever be fought for an obviously lost cause. There have been many cases in history when nations have gone to war knowing full well that they would lose. The leaders have felt that the nation's pride—or their personal honor—had to be upheld, even at the cost of much death and devastation. Under virtually any just war theory, that would be an unjust war.

What's more, the war must be limited to achieving the obtainable goal for which it is fought. A war may begin as a just war but then disintegrate into chaos and injustice. Once the goal has been obtained—or once it becomes clear that the goal cannot be obtained—the war must be brought to an end.

2. War must be the last resort. Whatever the dispute, every effort must be made to solve it peacefully before taking up arms. No matter how worthwhile the cause, killing people cannot be justified when the goal might be reached by peaceful means. Those means might include negotiation, diplomatic pressure, or economic boycotts.

3. The war must be fought by moral means. This condition puts limitations on the way wars can be fought. It forbids the use of any weapon or strategy that is immoral in and of itself. Most believers in a just war would define an immoral weapon as one that is so destructive that it inevitably kills large numbers of innocent people. Such weapons would include not only any large nuclear bomb or missile, but all kinds of chemical, biological, or other weapons that cannot be strictly targeted and controlled. An immoral strategy would include such things as terrorism against a civilian population, the poisoning of a community's water supply, and the deliberate bombing of cities.

The need to fight with moral means is the hardest condition of all for a modern war to meet. It assumes that a just war must be fought against military forces, not against civilians. Ideally, the war would be fought so that no civilians were killed or injured. There was a time when this might have been possible—when soldiers could meet on open battlefields and fight things out between themselves. But it is hard to imagine a major war being fought with modern weapons without large-scale death and injury to civilians. For pacifists, this impossibility means that no war can be considered truly just in the world today.

Even those who believe that a moral war can still be fought insist that provisions must be made for the noncombatants. They must be kept as safe as possible, and refugees caused by the war must be taken care of, not only during the war but afterward. No war can be considered just if it is fought without sufficient resources being applied to taking care of those who are injured or dispossessed by the results of that war.

4. The good effects of the war must outweigh the bad. Before it can be decided whether a war is just, the likely consequences of the war must be examined. How many people will die on each side? How many will be maimed? How many victims will be civilians? How many will be children? How many cities will be destroyed? How many families will be torn apart?

And, in the end, who will win? Even if your side wins, will the just goals you began with be accomplished? What unintended results might there be? Is the course the war will take predictable at all? Or, once started, is it likely to spread out of all control?

The answers to these questions must be weighed. When everything has been taken into account, the good that the war is likely to accomplish must outweigh the bad that it is sure to do.

What if one side abides by the conditions for a just war, but the other side violates them so badly that the effects of the war become so terrible that the evil being done far outweighs any possible good? Then, many just war supporters would argue, the war becomes unjust for both sides and must be ended.

On the face of it, this seems incredibly illogical and wrong. It means that the more brutal and immoral the other side is in fighting the war, the less just it is to fight that enemy. And yet, the defenders of the just war theory argue, this is the hard reality of war. If the results of fighting against an enemy will be worse than the results of not fighting the enemy, then the war should not be fought.

For those who believe in the just war theory, the conditions for a just war are not mere recommendations for civilized warfare. They are necessary requirements. If any one of them is not met, the war is not just and must not be fought.

Absolute pacifists, of course, reject all just war theories. They believe that *no* war is just, no matter how or why it is fought.

Rejecting Appeasement

In order to understand what peace commandos believe, it is also necessary to understand what they do not believe. They do not believe in appeasement, or giving in to unjust demands in order to avoid trouble. In 1938, for example, the leaders of several European countries tried to appease Adolf Hitler, who wanted to expand Germany's borders by taking territory away from weaker countries. Meeting in Munich, the leaders agreed to let Nazi Germany take over part of Czechoslovakia—against Czechoslovakia's will—in hopes that it would satisfy Hitler's appetite for other people's territory. It didn't, and the massive slaughter of World War II soon followed.

Some pacifists do become appeasers. They are so worried about the devastation of war that they are willing to try anything to avoid it—even accept the worst evil and injustice.

But peace commandos, like those we are talking about in this book, reject the idea of accepting evil as strongly as they reject the idea of war itself. They realize that, if war is unjust, then they must find other ways to fight.

Another Kind of Hero

Nonpacifists often assume that anyone who opposes violence is a coward. People who refuse to fight must be doing so because they are afraid of being hurt or killed. But this is not necessarily true.

No one denies the valor of the men and women of the U.S. armed forces. Everyone admires their bravery and their willingness to sacrifice their lives, if called on, to do what they see as their duty. Most Americans regard them as heroes. Thousands of books and films pay tribute to the warrior virtues of courage, strength, patriotism, and honor. But these virtues are not confined to the battlefield.

There are other heroes as well, heroes who fight in other ways, for other reasons. These are the brave men and women who believe in nonviolence, who dedicate their lives not to victory in war, but to the triumph of peace and justice. Peace commandos—pacifists and other nonviolent protestors—can be every bit as brave, strong, and honorable as any soldier. And as patriotic.

Like ordinary soldiers, they often have to pay a price for their beliefs. People who take a stand against war are often ridiculed and sometimes attacked. At best, they are considered foolish; at worst, dangerous. People identify them with the enemy and hate them for it. Antiwar demonstrators have been spit upon, teargassed, and beaten. Pacifists who refused to cooperate with their own nation's war machine have lost their jobs, been thrown into jail, and been branded as traitors. Some have been called upon to pay an even higher price—to pay, as Allison Krause did, the highest price that any warrior can pay.

One may agree with the peace commandos or disagree with them, but no one should doubt their courage. For the real peace commando, pacifism is not about escaping danger. It is about overcoming it. Pacifism is not about avoiding service to society. It is about embracing it. Pacifism is not about running away from war. It is about challenging the notion of war itself.

Chapter Two

As American As Apple Pie

United States history is often taught as a series of violent struggles. Americans are presented as forcibly overcoming a series of hostile obstacles and enemies. Taming the wilderness. Fighting for independence. Conquering the frontier. Subduing the "savages." Holding the Union together in the American Civil War. "Winning" the West. Waging gunboat diplomacy in Asia and carrying a "big stick" in the Americas. "Making the world safe for democracy" in the First World War and "liberating Europe" in the Second. Combatting Communist expansion in Korea and Vietnam. Wresting Middle Eastern oil from Iraq in the Gulf War. And so on.

The American tradition of war and violence is familiar to every schoolchild. But, although it is less well-known, pacifism has its own long tradition in American history.

Pacifism in the Colonies

The colony of Pennsylvania was founded by Quakers in the 1680s. Their leader, William Penn, considered the colony a "Holy Experiment" and did his best to establish a government built on principles of Christian love and brotherhood. He even named the capital city he founded Philadelphia, which means "brotherly love."

Penn and the Quakers were absolute pacifists. "We utterly deny all outward wars and strife, and fightings and outward weapons, for any end, or under any pretense whatever," they declared. "The spirit of Christ by which we are guided, is not changeable. . . . Therefore, we cannot learn war any more."[1]

The Quakers put their radical beliefs into action dealing with the Native Americans. Almost alone among the colonists, the Pennsylvanians protected the Indians' human rights under colonial law. Pennsylvania recognized the Native Americans' ownership of the land and insisted that they be paid for it. While colonists elsewhere subdued them by force, Penn made a treaty of friendship with them.

The Quakers' peaceful ways proved extraordinarily successful. As long as Penn was alive, there was no trouble between Indians and colonists, and Pennsylvania was one of the most prosperous of all the colonies.[2]

The Quakers were not the only pacifists in colonial America. Other peace churches included the Mennonites, the Brethren, and the Schwekenfelders. Their members would not take part in the militia or in the occasional fighting that erupted against the Indians. Some colonies respected the pacifists' religious beliefs, but others fined them, or even threw them into prison for refusing to join in the defense of the settlements.

Most members of the peace churches wouldn't take active part in the American Revolution either, although some helped supply the revolutionaries with food and clothes. Those who refused to help were sometimes dealt with harshly by the revolutionaries.

Pacifism in the Early United States

American pacifists hoped the founding of the United States would assure peace. Representatives of the people would meet to settle differences between groups within the nation, so there would be no cause for civil war, while the great expanse of the Atlantic Ocean would help protect against foreign invasion. Besides, foreign wars, most people believed, were caused by disputes between kings or the desire to expand empires. The United States would have neither a monarch nor an empire. Except for occasional problems with Indian tribes, military conflict seemed unlikely to trouble the new nation. The War of 1812 soon shattered that happy illusion, presenting American pacifists with the first 19th-century challenge to their beliefs.

Conscription was considered unconstitutional in the early United States, so there was no national draft. Some of the states, however, did conscript men into the military. Others imposed taxes to help pay for the war. The pacifists, of course, refused to serve. Many refused to pay taxes as well. In some places, their property was taken away from them.

Following the war, many Americans reexamined their beliefs. It was now obvious that the United States would not be safe from war, monarch or no monarch, ocean or no ocean. Even many Americans who were not pacifists became convinced that some better way was needed to solve international disputes. They began organizing what they called peace societies.

Small groups sprang up in communities around the country. These formed the base of the larger American Peace Society, which was founded in 1828 by a Maine merchant and ex-sea captain named William Ladd. The American Peace Society called for a Congress of Nations and Court of Nations that would establish an international rule of law that applied to all countries. This would provide a separate, fair, and, most important of all, nonmilitary way to settle quarrels between nations.

By the late 1830s, however, arguments within the peace movement caused a split in the American Peace Society. Everyone in the peace movement wanted nations to resolve disputes nonviolently, but what if they didn't? What happens when a rogue nation attacks a peaceful neighbor? Or when some ruthless empire, bent on conquest, begins to gobble up other nations by force? Most members of the American Peace Society felt that force was sometimes justified in cases like these. A smaller group known as the *ultraists* opposed war under any circumstances at all. Led by the great antislavery campaigner William Lloyd Garrison, the ultraists broke away from the American Peace Society and founded their own organization, the Non-Resistance Society.

The Non-Resisters based their extreme beliefs on an interpretation of Christian principles. They opposed all forms of violence, including capital punishment and taking up arms in self-defense. The most radical of them, like Garrison, saw all governmental authority as a form of violence. This led them to oppose any appeal to governmental power, even lawsuits that called on the government to take property away from the loser.

Opposing the Mexican War

In 1846, the United States went to war with Mexico over ownership of Texas. Mexico did not recognize Texas's claim of independence, and was outraged when the United States made Texas a state. The war began when Mexican troops attacked a U.S. military patrol along the Rio Grande. It was little more than a skirmish along a disputed border, but President James Polk treated it as a mini-invasion.

"War exists by act of Mexico itself," declared the president. "Mexico . . . has shed American blood upon the American soil."[3] A move to declare war passed the House and the Senate by a combined vote of 214 to 16. The war was just as popular with ordinary citizens, who delighted in seeing the United States expand into the West. Southerners were particularly happy, because Texas was being welcomed into the Union as a slave state.

For most Americans, the Mexican conflict was an easy war to like. Morally, going to war seemed more than justified by the Mexican attack. There was no threat to American territory outside of Texas, and because there was no military draft, no one was being forced to fight. In fact, the young men who went to war were volunteers eager for adventure.

But not all Americans welcomed the war. Some members of the Whig party protested what they believed to be an unconstitutional war of conquest against Mexico. Most of the opponents, however, were against the expansion of slavery. They saw the war as a backdoor attempt to spread the hated institution of slavery into the West.

This was something new in the history of antiwar activity in the United States. Suddenly, the pacifists who opposed all wars were joined in protest by significant numbers of Americans who opposed this war in particular. The new antiwar forces did not object to fighting Mexico because they opposed war. They objected because they thought the U.S. government was in the wrong.

Many of the protestors denounced the war in the strongest possible terms. Senator Tom Corwin from Ohio identified himself with the Mexican enemy. "If I were a Mexican," he declared, "I would tell you, 'Have you not room in your own country to bury your dead men? If you come into mine, we will greet you with bloody hands and welcome you to hospitable graves.'"[4]

Some of the most respected figures in American history stood up among the dissenters. A congressman from Illinois named Abraham Lincoln was one of the war's most bitter critics in the House. Frederick Douglass, the escaped slave who became an eloquent abolitionist author, railed against the war in the pages of his newspaper *North Star.*

Abolitionist writers like Douglass were bound to oppose the war, but speaking out against a popular war took a particular kind of courage for politicians like Lincoln and Corwin. They were attacked in the press as traitors. Lincoln was one of those who paid a price for his opposition to the war. Though he eventually voted to supply the American soldiers in the field, his attacks on the war cost him the respect and support of many voters back in Illinois.

Henry David Thoreau's "Peaceable Revolution"

Of all the protests sparked by the Mexican War, none would have a more lasting impact than that of Henry David Thoreau. No one could be more American than Thoreau. Born and bred in Massachusetts, he was a New England Yankee through and through. A friend and companion of the philosopher Ralph Waldo Emerson, Thoreau was the author of the classic nature study *Walden.*

He was also an abolitionist who was so outraged by the Mexican War that, as the editors of *The Democracy Reader* described his reaction, "he personally seceded from the union . . . refusing to pay his taxes to carry on what he regarded as an unjust war."[5] Thoreau was briefly jailed for refusing to pay taxes, but he continued to withhold his taxes even after the war was over, in protest against the government's tolerance of slavery.

Thoreau explained his reasons for defying the government in an oration and essay called *Civil Disobedience.*[6] If the essay had simply attacked the Mexican War, it would hardly be remembered today. But it went beyond an attack on the government's policy. Thoreau not only prescribed action for those citizens who opposed that policy to take, he insisted that it was their duty to place their own consciences above the demands of their government.

"That government is best that governs not at all," argued Thoreau. "And when men are prepared for it, that will be the kind of government which they will have." In the meantime, even the best government is little more than a necessary evil. "The objections which have been brought against a standing army, and they are many and weighty and deserve to prevail, may also at last be brought against a standing government. The standing army is only an arm of the standing government. The government itself . . . is equally liable to be abused and perverted. . . . Witness the present Mexican War."

Most people, Thoreau complained, let the government make their moral decisions for them.

> The mass of men serve the State thus, not as men mainly, but as machines, with their bodies. They are the standing army, the militia, jailers . . . etc. In most cases, there is no free exercise whatever of the judgment or of the moral sense; but they put themselves on a level with wood and earth and stones. . . . They have the same sort of worth only as horses and dogs. Yet such as these even are commonly esteemed good citizens. Others, as most legislators, politicians, lawyers, ministers, and office-holders, serve the state chiefly with their heads; and, as they rarely make any moral distinctions, they are as likely to serve the devil, without *intending* it, as God.

Only "a very few . . . heroes, patriots, martyrs, reformers in the great sense, and *men,* serve the State with their consciences also," declared Thoreau. Those few, he went on, usually serve not by obeying the government, but by resisting it. As a result, "they are commonly treated by it as enemies."

But doesn't the citizen have a duty to obey the law, even when the law is wrong? "Why has every man a conscience, then?" asked Thoreau. "I think that we should be men first and subjects afterward. It is not desirable to cultivate a respect for the law, as much as for the right. The only obligation which I have a right to assume, is to do at any time what I think right."

For Thoreau, obedience to an unjust authority—including giving financial or other support to an unjust war—robbed the individual of something vital to human nature:

Law never made man a whit more just; and by means of their respect for it, even the well disposed are daily made the agents of injustice. A common and natural result of an undue respect for law is, that you may see a file of soldiers, colonel, captain, corporal, privates, powder monkeys and all, marching in admirable order over hill and dale to the wars, against their wills, aye, against their common sense and consciences, which makes it very

steep marching indeed, and produces a palpi-
tation of the heart. They have no doubt that it
is a damnable business with which they are
concerned; they are all peaceably inclined.
Now, what are they? Men at all? or small mov-
able forts and magazines, at the service of
some unscrupulous man in power?

What is a citizen to do when faced with a government
that does wrong? "It is not a man's duty, as a matter of course,
to devote himself to the eradication of . . . even the most enormous wrong," admitted Thoreau. "But it is his duty, at least, to
wash his hands of it." Thoreau washed his hands of the Mexican War by refusing to pay his taxes.

But Thoreau wasn't just interested in keeping his
hands clean. He wanted to end the war and to end slavery as
well. But what could he do? Not only the government but the
majority of the public favored the war, and most people tol-
erated slavery as well. What could the minority who opposed
them do?

They could refuse to cooperate with the government
in its unjust policies, even to the point of going to prison if
necessary:

Under a government which imprisons any unjustly, the true place for a just man is also a prison . . . where the State places those who are not *with* her, but *against* her,—the only house in a slave state in which a free man can abide with honor. If any think that their influence would be lost there, and their voices no longer afflict the ear of the State, that they would not be as an enemy within its walls, they do not know by how much truth is stronger than error. A minority is powerless while it conforms to the majority; it is not even a minority then; but it is irresistible when it clogs by its whole weight. If the alternative is to keep all just men in prison, or give up war and slavery, the State will not hesitate which to choose. If a thousand men were not to pay their tax-bills this year, that would not be a violent and bloody measure, as it would be to pay them, and enable the State to commit violence and shed innocent blood. This is, in fact, the definition of a peaceable revolution, if any such is possible.

When a law is unjust, argued Thoreau, good people should disobey it. If enough people refuse to cooperate with an unjust government, the unjust government itself will ultimately collapse. This was the heart of Thoreau's argument, and the key to the enormous effect his little essay would have: the idea that a minority with right on its side could triumph over the combined might of the government and the majority of the public put together. This idea would inspire movements for peace and justice around the world.

Less than a century after Thoreau's death, his idea would show Mohandas Gandhi how to free India from its British masters. It would teach Martin Luther King, Jr., how to break the bonds of racial separation in the United States. And it would give strength to the peaceable revolutionaries who freed Eastern Europe from the domination of the Soviet Union.

For all its international influence, however, Thoreau's argument was as American as apple pie. It was rooted in the fundamental American ideals of individual freedom, self-reliance, and personal conscience.

Chapter Three

Three Who Worked *for* Peace *and* Justice

P acifists have always recognized that working for peace involves more than not fighting wars. As the Quaker suffragist Lucretia Mott explained more than a century ago, "There can be no true peace that is not founded on justice and right."[1]

At the same time, not all peace commandos begin as pacifists. Like the three people described in this chapter, many are driven to oppose war because of their belief in other causes—particularly a deep concern for the poor. Although different in many ways, they all followed a similar path, moving on from a concern for social and economic justice "to extend works of mercy into works of peace."[2]

In America, at least, pacifism and a desire for social reform have often gone hand in hand. People who work to make the world a better place for people to live naturally hate the death, devastation, and misery brought about by war. For their part, most pacifists recognize that working for peace involves more than opposing wars that have already started.

51

In the early 20th century, the American peace movement was made up largely of reformers who combined the struggle for peace with the struggle to overcome injustice. Many believed that the rich and the powerful ran society for their own benefit. The working poor were exploited by employers who paid them less than their labor was worth and pocketed the difference for themselves. In the days before unemployment insurance and government welfare measures, those unfit to work were left to beg or starve to death along with their families.

The social workers, labor leaders, and others who rebelled at these conditions saw most wars as disputes between the rich and the powerful interests—monarchs, empires, financiers, business tycoons, and corporations—that had little to do with the welfare of ordinary people. Reformers who spent their lives trying to help the poor had no wish to see those people slaughtered to increase the wealth of arms manufacturers and the size of empires.

Jane Addams

No American woman was more identified with both social causes and the cause of peace than Jane Addams of Chicago.

Addams was recognized as one of the most remarkable people of her time, man or woman. "Her mind," said one admirer, "had more 'floor space' in it than any other I have known."[3]

Addams combined a deep belief in the principles of Christian morality with a tireless dedication to social reforms. For her, they were the same. As a young woman, she and a friend had converted an aging Chicago mansion into an experiment in social reform called Hull House. Its first function was as a settlement house, a refuge in which desperate immigrants could make the adjustment to their new land. Hull House also served as a center for social research, adding to the understanding of poverty and its effects on people and neighborhoods. The success of Hull House made it a model for similar settlement houses across the country.

At a time when women were expected to keep quiet about political affairs, Jane Addams spoke out on every issue. And she was not satisfied with talk. She believed in action. She was a leader in the fight for woman suffrage. But she wanted women to do more than vote. She wanted them to take the lead in transforming society. By the turn of the 20th century, she was the best-known political activist in Chicago.

At a time when corrupt political bosses ran the city, she fought their efforts to take advantage of Chicago's immigrants. At a time when labor unions were considered radical, if not unconstitutional, she campaigned for union rights and demanded better working conditions in the factories. At a time when poor children worked ten-hour days at the age of ten, she campaigned for an end to child labor and for education for every child.

Addams was a longtime member of the American Peace Society because she believed that pacifism was a natural ally of woman suffrage and social reform. By the time World War I broke out in Europe in 1914, however, the American Peace Society had become a relatively conservative organization. As the war went on, many of its members even became convinced that the United States should join the war on the Allied side. But not Jane Addams. She was convinced that the United States should stay out of what seemed to be a senseless European quarrel.

Addams was wise enough to know that war leads to repression. In wartime, governments silence their critics. People like herself, who attacked the way things were done in the country, would be treated as dangerous distractions from the war effort. Besides, there was too much still to do for poor people in America to waste precious resources on killing poor people in Europe.

Dissatisfied with the American Peace Society, Addams helped found two new antiwar organizations. The most important was the Women's Peace Party (WPP), which got many of its members from the woman suffrage movement. The WPP argued that giving women the right to vote would help bring peace to the world. Its members believed that women were more peaceable by nature and would use the power of the ballot to promote candidates who would work for peace. Few women were actually candidates themselves, of course, since at that time women couldn't even vote in most parts of the country. Those who did run tended to support the cause of peace. When it came time for Congress to vote on entering World War I, the one woman in Congress, Jeannette Rankin of Montana, would vote against entering the war. "I want to stand by my country," she said. "But I cannot vote for war."[4]

For a time, the WPP was a very active American peace organization. Along with other groups, it held rallies, staged "peace parades," and did everything it could to educate people about the horrors of war and the need for peace.

In 1916, many of the most energetic social reformers launched a new organization called the American Union Against Militarism. By that time, much of the country was preparing for war. Led by a bright, energetic, and talented young woman named Crystal Eastman, the union was more radical than the Women's Peace Party. Among other things, it held rallies in many cities, urging the country to refuse to prepare itself for war. The union also spoke out against conscription (the draft).

Things changed in 1917, when the United States actually entered the war. As usual when a war begins, the country was swept with a wave of war fervor. Most Americans rushed to support the war effort. Many of the more traditional social reformers cut down their antiwar activities. Others eliminated them altogether. Some were afraid of the growing government crackdown on antiwar protests. But others, including Jane Addams, downplayed their antiwar views because public opinion had turned so strongly in favor of the war that they feared a backlash against all social reform if the reformers were identified too closely with pacifism. While they continued to oppose the war, they did so more quietly, letting others like Crystal Eastman carry on the public fight.[5]

No longer able to fight effectively against the war, Jane Addams did her best to lessen its horrors. She threw herself into humanitarian efforts to help the victims of the war and into forward-looking plans for an international conference after the war was over.

In 1931, she was awarded a Nobel Peace Prize, along with Nicholas Murray Butler, a leader in the push for disarmament after World War I.

Eugene V. Debs and the Radical Labor Movement

Like Jane Addams, Eugene V. Debs spent his life working to improve the lives of others. But Debs worked in a very different way. He was a labor organizer who began his career enlisting the poorly paid men who worked for the railroads into a union. Only by joining together, the union men believed, could the workers become strong enough to bargain equally with the powerful owners of the mighty railroads.

Virtually the only weapon the workers had in the uneven battle with their employers was the strike. But, when Debs's union struck the Pullman Car Company in 1894, the workers found themselves facing more than their bosses. They found themselves facing the federal government as well, when President Grover Cleveland called out federal troops to put down the strike and force the workers back on the job.

Debs was thrown into jail for six months. He came out a hero to American workers, and a committed Socialist. He was convinced that the government needed to stop protecting the interests of the wealthy people who owned the great business corporations and to protect the rights of the workers instead. As a Socialist, he wanted the government to actually take over the ownership of much of American industry on behalf of the people, running it for the people's benefit instead of to make profits for a handful of businessmen.

More determined than ever to help the workers, Debs helped organize a radical new union, the Industrial Workers of the World (IWW). Instead of appealing to workers in one company or trade, like most unions of the time, the IWW set out to organize all industrial workers. It quickly established itself as the most aggressive labor organization in the United States. Wherever there was trouble between workers and employers, "Wobblies"—as IWW members were known—showed up to encourage the workers to carry on the fight. Altogether, the militant union conducted at least 150 strikes.

Believing that union activity alone was not enough to make the United States a just society, Debs became the presidential candidate of the Socialist party in 1900. He would be renominated four times. At the time the Great War (as World War I was then known) broke out in Europe, Debs was the leading Socialist voice in the United States.

The Socialists opposed war in general, and the Great War in particular. While most people accepted wars as conflicts between nations, the Socialists saw everything in terms of conflicts between social classes. They believed that the real conflict in the world was between the small class of wealthy

and powerful capitalists who controlled the world's governments and the much larger class of workers and their families
the capitalists exploited. Wars were a distraction from this,
the most fundamental struggle.

Wars were quarrels between capitalists. The workers
had no stake in them. Worse, wars tended to divide working
people, setting them against one another and diverting them
from their struggle with the real enemies, the capitalists who
exploited them all. "The master class has always declared the
wars," proclaimed Debs, but "the subject class has always
fought the battles."[6]

The Socialists were not much interested in joining the
older peace groups, and the traditional groups were not very
interested in having them.[7] The two camps opposed war for
different reasons. Besides, several important members of the
traditional groups were prominent capitalists themselves.
The World Peace Foundation had been founded by the
wealthy publisher Edwin Ginn, who even talked about running the peace movement like a business. The fabulously rich
Andrew Carnegie had donated $10 million of his own money
to establish the Carnegie Endowment for International Peace,
even though he had made his fortune in the steel industry,
which stood to profit from any war. Perhaps the most visible
of all the opponents of the Great War was the automobile

tycoon Henry Ford. In late 1915, Ford hired his own ocean liner and sailed more than 100 pacifists to Europe in an attempt to negotiate an end to the fighting.

Debs and the Socialists considered rich capitalists like Ford and Carnegie enemies, and rejected their ways of campaigning for peace. While the traditional peace movement wanted to work for peace through negotiation, the Socialists and other radicals favored a policy of direct action and resistance against any possible war effort.

In 1917, a group of radicals founded the People's Council of America for Democracy and Peace. Inspired by the Communist Revolution, which even then was overthrowing the government of Russia, the People's Council saw itself as a kind of shadow government. It claimed to express "the will of the people" for peace much better than the real government, which was "organized for the conduct of war."[8]

Whatever the will of the people had been before, once the United States actually entered the war most Americans rallied to support the "boys" going "over there" to fight in Europe. The radical antiwar forces shrank to a small and weak minority.

The labor movement as a whole was divided over the war. The radical unions like the IWW continued to oppose it, but moderate union leaders like Samuel Gompers of the

American Federation of Labor (AFL) turned out to be undependable allies in the cause of peace. Gompers had participated in peace groups before the war, but he had silenced his pacifism once the guns began to roar in Europe. Now that the United States had joined the war, Gompers turned around entirely and supported the war.

Radicals like Debs concentrated most of their efforts on fighting the Selective Service Act of 1917, which required young men to serve in the war if they were conscripted. This put them in direct conflict not only with government policy, but with the law. Peace activists who advised young draftees to refuse to enter the military were breaking the law. In the eyes of the government, they were no longer mere dissenters, they were criminals.

Several peace leaders, including Debs, were tried and convicted for their antiwar and anticonscription activities. Already in his 60s, Debs was sentenced to ten years in prison. By 1920, the war in Europe was over, but Debs was still in prison. Nonetheless, the Socialists nominated Debs for president again. Even though he was forced to campaign from his prison cell, Debs won the votes of 919,799 of his fellow citizens—more than he had ever won before.

Prison was hard on Debs's aging body, but it could not touch his spirit. He was convinced that his cause was just. In spirit, he would later write, "I was never more free in my life . . . than I was in that prison cell."[9]

Debs was eventually released from prison by order of the Republican president Warren G. Harding in 1921. He spent his few remaining years in poor health, beloved by the union members for whom he had fought all his life and honored even by his enemies as a man of great nobility who was willing to sacrifice everything for what he believed.

In fact, although the United States and its allies had won the Great War, the unprecedented slaughter left a bad taste in many Americans' mouths. Debs, Addams, and other pacifists were eventually as respected for their stand against American entry into the war as they were once ridiculed for it.

Dorothy Day and the Catholic Worker Movement

Dorothy Day was born in 1897, the daughter of a sportswriter father and a mother who worked as a stenographer. When she was a child, her middle-class family suffered financial setbacks and moved to Chicago. In later life, she remembered being ashamed of the family's poor circumstances and of having to live in an apartment over a saloon.

While still a teenager, she discovered both a desire to write and a "call" to work for social justice for the poor. She quit college in 1916 to become a writer for left-wing papers and magazines that took prolabor and Socialist stands on many issues. In her spare time, she demonstrated in favor of woman suffrage and against United States participation in World War I. Politically, her sympathies were always with the rebels—the Socialists, Communists, and anarchists. She even joined the radical IWW.

Writing for the *Masses*, the best-known of all the left-wing magazines, she got to know many of the most colorful literary and artistic figures of the early 20th century, including famous writers like novelist John Dos Passos and playwright Eugene O'Neill. As young as she was, she must have been impressed with being in such lofty company. But even literary giants did not intimidate her when her deep sense of right and wrong was violated. Once, when eating at a restaurant, a *Masses* editor used the term *nigger*. An outraged Day stood up and loudly informed him that if he used it again, she would slap his face.[10]

When she was 19 years old, Day was arrested for taking part in a woman suffrage demonstration in front of the White House. She was kicked and beaten by the police and lit-

erally thrown into jail. It was her first taste of real violence—
the kind that the striking workers and political radicals she
sympathized with faced all the time—and it shook her badly.
She felt humiliated and ashamed. Debs felt "free" in his jail
cell, but Day felt as if she "would never be free again."[11]

Released from jail, Day was shaken but stubbornly
determined to be true to her beliefs. Unwilling to take a job
that would contribute to the war effort in any way, she honored her conscience by working as a hospital nurse until the
war was over.

Day was picked up by federal agents in a raid on an
IWW boardinghouse. Mistaken for a prostitute, she was
thrown into jail again. This imprisonment was even harder
than the first. She felt an even deeper sense of shame at being
punished as a prostitute, even though she had done nothing
to deserve it. What's more, she began to question the depth
of her own commitment to the poor. She talked and wrote
about their suffering but rarely shared it, as she was doing
now. Did she have the stomach to do more? She wasn't sure.

Day worked as a journalist until the sale of a book man-
uscript to the movies enabled her to move to an artist's
colony on Staten Island. She fell in love with an English anar-
chist and lived with him in what she always thought of as a
common-law marriage. At the age of 29, she had a daughter

she named Tamar Theresa. The miracle of Tamar's birth made her think more deeply than ever before about the meaning of human life. She began reading books about philosophy and religion. Telling a friend that she was "turned on religiously" by her readings,[12] she converted to the Roman Catholic church.

Day now began writing mostly for liberal Catholic magazines like *Commonweal* and *America*. Through these articles, she met a French intellectual named Paul Maurin. Like Day, Maurin was both a Catholic and a left-wing political radical. This was an unusual combination at a time when most Christian pacifists belonged to one of the Protestant peace churches, while most leftist radicals were atheists. More and more, Day found herself in conflict with her atheist friends and even with her common-law husband. They could not understand her new faith. "Is it not possible to protest, to expose, to complain, to point out abuses and demand reforms without desiring the overthrow of religion?" asked Day in an editorial.[13]

Maurin thought it was. He helped her understand how their faith could be combined with socialism. In 1933, he convinced her to found a reform-minded newspaper they called the *Catholic Worker*. Day described it as a paper for the unemployed, and there were plenty of unemployed to read it. This was the decade of the Great Depression, and the little paper's circulation soared. By 1936, it rose to 150,000.[14] The paper's success made no difference to Day or Maurin financially. The unemployed had no money, and the price was kept at a penny a copy. Thousands of copies were just given away.

The *Catholic Worker* became the inspiration and rallying point for a new kind of social action. Determined that she would not just write about her beliefs—she would live them—Day opened her own house to homeless poor people. She and the paper's staff began distributing food and clothing to the poor along with free newspapers. Before long, 30 similar "houses of hospitality" were operating around the country, along with several communal farms established by followers of Day and Maurin. The *Catholic Worker* was no longer just a publication. It had become a movement.

Pacifism and nonviolence were important elements in that movement. "The emphasis was always, from the very beginning, on the use of nonviolence as a way of changing the social order," Day explained in the late 1960s. The objective, she went on, "was to try to work so as to bring about the kind of a society where it is easy to be good."[15] And that required, among many other conditions, a society at peace: "The emphasis of the *Catholic Worker* has been, from the beginning, in each and every war—beginning with the

Chinese-Japanese War and then the Ethiopian War, and the Spanish Civil War, the Second World War and the Korean War, the Algerian War—it's been always on nonviolence. And we've always emphasized the necessity of developing a love of enemy as well as a love of brother."[16]

The influence of the Catholic Worker movement has been enormous, both on the movement for social justice and on the American peace movement. Among those who learned something of the reality of poverty and nonviolence from Day and her "houses of hospitality" were a young Catholic politician named John Kennedy and a writer named Michael Harrington. Harrington, who once edited the *Catholic Worker,* later wrote *The Other America,* a landmark book on poverty in America, which would inspire President John Kennedy to launch the War on Poverty programs of the 1960s.[17] The Catholic Worker movement's influence would be equally dramatic on the generation of antiwar activists who fought against the war in Vietnam.

Ultimately, however, Day's most lasting influence was in opening up the American Catholic church to a new concern for poverty and peace. Before Day converted to Catholicism, the Catholic church in America had been unsympathetic to pacifism, if not positively hostile to it. Many American Catholics were either first-, second-, or third-generation immigrants, eager to prove their patriotism with military service.

Officially, the Church taught that war was a result of sin, but it permitted Catholics to fight in just wars. (This is still the Church's official position.) In practice, Catholic authorities in most countries, including the United States, usually encouraged Catholics to accept any war the government entered as just. Certainly, American Church officials had never encouraged or even authorized young Catholics to resist military service the way some Protestant denominations did. Day, however, found pacifism in the teachings of the Church. In doing so, she helped many other Catholics to find it there, too.

Driven by a bitter hatred and fear of Communism, most Church officials continued to support American military efforts throughout the cold war. But growing numbers of ordinary Catholics were moved by Dorothy Day's Catholic Worker movement. In 1983, the American Catholic bishops, who speak for the Catholic church in the United States, issued an historic pastoral letter entitled "The Challenge of Peace: God's Promise and Our Response." It condemned the nuclear arms race and seemed to many Catholics to move the Church a giant step toward pacifism.

The Catholic church is still not a peace church in the

way that the Mennonite, Quaker, and Brethren churches are. But it is no longer hostile to the ideal of pacifism, nor to the practice of conscientious objection. Lay Catholics, priests, nuns, and Catholic organizations like Pax Christi have been in the forefront of recent peace activities in the United States. Much of the credit for this transformation goes to the Catholic Worker movement and its founder. As one Catholic bishop has said, "Dorothy Day has transformed the Catholic Church in America more than anyone."[18]

Chapter Four

In Times
of
War

H istorically, peace movements tend to be at their biggest and loudest during times of peace, and weakest during times of war. There are exceptions, including the massive outpouring of protest against the war in Vietnam, but most often wars splinter peace groups and drain them of members. Before World War I, for example, the peace movement claimed millions of supporters. Once the United States entered the war, the vast majority of them disappeared.

It's relatively easy for many people to reject the idea of war during times of peace. After all, everybody wants peace, don't they? Once one's country is actually at war, however, even many peacetime pacifists find themselves swept up in the war fever that sweeps through the nation. When the whole society is mobilizing to fight, people find it difficult to stand against the tide.

In wartime, people see the choices differently. Once the troops are in the field and the bombers in the air, the choice that people see is no longer a question of war or peace. It is a question of us or them. To side with peace seems almost like siding with the enemy, and that is something few people want to do.

What is more, the personal stakes become higher. In peacetime, people are relatively free to take any position they choose. But in wartime, governments tend to crack down on peace activists. Before the war begins, campaigning for peace may make you unpopular. Your neighbors may consider you naive, and the government may consider you a nuisance. But once your country is fighting, your neighbors may hate you and the government may consider you a traitor. It might even throw you into jail.

Choosing between Evils

The first war to seriously divide American pacifists was the Civil War. Most of the pacifists were also strong abolitionists. Always before, the causes of peace and abolition had seemed to go together. The abolitionists had opposed the Mexican War both because it was war and because it would help spread slavery into the West. But the Civil War presented them with an impossible choice. Which was the greater good, peace or freedom? Which was the greater evil, war or slavery?

It was the old question of a just war. The cause was good—but did the good that might be accomplished outweigh the damage the war would do? For better or worse, most abolitionists decided that it did. They put aside their hatred of war in favor of their desire to free the slaves. Among them was no less a leader than William Lloyd Garrison himself—the radical pacifist who had founded the Non-Resistance Society. Garrison and many other prewar pacifists ended up pressing their fellow abolitionists to abandon their devotion to nonviolence until the war was over and the slaves were free. This marked the first time that the American peace movement was splintered by such a choice. But it would not be the last.

Labor and World War I

World War I presented a different kind of challenge to the pacifist beliefs of American union leaders. While Eugene Debs and the Socialists insisted that all workers were brothers and should refuse to fight one another no matter which countries they came from, moderate labor leaders like Samuel Gompers enthusiastically embraced the war effort.

Gompers and the other moderates founded a prowar organization called the American Alliance for Labor and Democracy to compete with the Socialists' People's Council. The alliance worked to persuade American workers to support the war, and to convince other Americans that the labor movement was as patriotic as anyone else. "This is Labor's War," declared an alliance publication.[1] By supporting it, the moderate labor movement hoped to be recognized as full partners with business and government in the American dream.

For a short time, the People's Council and the American Alliance waged their own war for the loyalty of the American labor movement. The alliance won. This was partly because of disagreement within the People's Council itself. But there were other reasons, too. Emotionally, it was hard for workers to oppose a war in which their own sons and brothers were fighting and dying on foreign battlefields. Economically, it was hard for them to oppose a war that brought an upsurge in industrial production and more jobs for American workers.

The Peace Movement between the Wars

The United States and its allies won the Great War, but the extent of the war's destruction disillusioned many Americans with the whole idea of war. A generation of young European men had been decimated, an entire continent had been devastated, countries and empires had been torn apart, and many of the world's major countries had been plunged into debt. Worst of all, for the first time in history, war casualties were numbered not in the thousands, or even in the millions, but in the tens of millions. "And for what?" asked an American columnist. "Would it have been any worse if Germany had won?. . . No one knows," he concluded.[2]

Revulsion at the Great War led to the biggest peace movement yet in the United States. People were eager for new, nonviolent ways to solve problems. They urged the United States to join the new international organization, the League of Nations, and to submit international disputes to the newly formed World Court.

Peace groups appealed to people of all kinds. The American League against War and Fascism rallied left-wingers of all varieties to the peace movement. Jane Addams's Women's Peace party became the Women's International League for Peace and Freedom and attracted more than

13,000 women to the cause.[3] The Fellowship of Reconciliation, led for a time by the brilliant A. J. Muste, united pacifist Protestants, while Dorothy Day's Catholic Worker movement attracted similar-thinking Catholics. At one time, an umbrella organization called the National Council for the Prevention of War served as a voice and clearinghouse for some 31 antiwar groups. Its spokeswoman in Washington, D.C., was Jeannette Rankin, who had earlier been the first woman ever to serve in Congress.

Estimates of the number of pacifists in the 1930s ranged as high as 12 million—or one out of every ten Americans.[4] But then came World War II.

The Effect of World War II

No major war ever presented as difficult a dilemma for pacifists as World War II. The Nazis were so terrible—so determined to swallow up country after country, so vicious in their slaughter of innocent civilians—that it was almost impossible not to support military action against them. Then, with war sentiment already growing in the United States, the Japanese attacked Pearl Harbor. Could the United States sit back and do nothing? Even the great majority of the 12 million prewar pacifists decided something had to be done.

The peace churches continued to urge their members not to fight. Church-related organizations like the Quakers' American Friends Service Committee gave aid and comfort to conscientious objectors, as did the secular (nonreligious) War Resisters League. But groups like these were almost alone in opposing the war.

World War II went a long way toward discrediting pacifism altogether. After the war, the death camps were discovered in places like Auschwitz and Buchenwald, where the Nazis had murdered millions of Jews, Gypsies, Poles, homosexuals, and others they considered enemies. For many people, the death camps revealed the full extent of Nazi evil and proved that the war had been more than justified.

Some observers, like the liberal columnist Walter Lippmann, even blamed pacifists for causing the horrors of World War II in the first place. "They were the cause of the failure to keep pace with the growth of German and Japanese armaments,"[5] charged Lippmann. He and other critics lumped all pacifists together with the appeasers, ignoring the fact that pacifists like Rabbi Stephen Wise and the Reverend John Haymes Holmes had been among the earliest voices to warn against the Nazis and their poisonous anti-Semitism.[6]

World War I had spurred the growth of the American

peace movement after the war, but World War II had the opposite effect. The enormous success of American military power in the war—capped off by the explosions of two atomic weapons over Japan—did even more to weaken pacifism's appeal. People were less attracted to peace when they felt that they could win any war.

For more than a decade after the atom bombs had been dropped on Hiroshima and Nagasaki, what relatively little peace activity existed focused on the need to rid the world of the awesomely destructive new weapons. Old groups like the War Resisters League and new ones like the National Committee for a Sane Nuclear Policy (SANE), attracted many people to the cause of nuclear disarmament, but they did nothing to halt the buildup of nuclear weapon stockpiles by the United States and the Soviet Union. It would take the terribly unpopular war in Vietnam to reawaken a broad-based peace movement in the United States.

Chapter Five

"We Shall Not Be Moved"

F or the peace commandos, pacifism is not merely an opposition to war. It is an alternative to war. Nonpacifists often mistake pacifism for laziness, or even indifference. They assume that unwillingness to fight for a cause means unwillingness to work for it. But, for the peace commandos, nothing could be further from the truth. For them, nonviolence is not a way of avoiding action, but of taking it.

"Pacifism is not passivity," insists Coleman McCarthy of the Center for Teaching Peace. Pacifism doesn't even mean rejecting force, says McCarthy. It means choosing a different kind of force. "Those who choose nonviolent force opt for the force of justice, the force of love, the force of sharing wealth, the force of ideas, the force of organized defiance to corrupt power. Fighting with those kinds of forces is the essence of nonviolence."[1]

In his essay on civil disobedience, Thoreau told the world a great secret: that nonviolence could be a powerful weapon. But Thoreau could only reveal the secret. He couldn't prove it. That was left to Mohandas Gandhi to do nearly a century later.

Even a book, like this one, that focuses on the American peace movement has to acknowledge the example of Gandhi. It was Gandhi who showed that the ideas that the pacifists had always preached could be turned into effective action in the real world of clubs and bullets. It was Gandhi who made Thoreau's "peaceable revolution" a reality.

Gandhi

Gandhi was born and raised in India but went to England as a young man to study law. Oddly, for a man who would challenge an empire and make a revolution, he was not a bold man by nature. He was so shaken by his first appearance in court that he couldn't even talk. Nonetheless, he was a good enough lawyer to get a job representing an Indian company in South Africa in 1893.

Gandhi soon discovered that Indians in South Africa were subjected to a variety of racial indignities. He was so offended by this mistreatment that he determined to resist South Africa's system of racial discrimination. The man who had been too timid to speak up in court somehow found the strength to lead South Africa's Indian community in protest against their treatment by the white society.

A devoted reader, Gandhi had been deeply affected by the ideas of Thoreau and of the Russian pacifist Leo Tolstoy, who had written *War and Peace* and other monumental works. Gandhi took their ideas and refined them, coming up with a policy of nonviolent resistance that he called satyagraha. A Sanskrit word meaning a combination of truth and firmness, satyagraha might be translated as "the force of truth."

Gandhi was a deeply religious Hindu, and satyagraha was as much a spiritual force as a political one. He called on his people to reform themselves spiritually before reforming society. He told them they must learn self-control and discipline, then follow a strict policy of nonviolence while acting together in refusing to cooperate with South Africa's racial policies. If necessary, he told them, they must be willing to be beaten or imprisoned rather than accept the discrimination imposed by the white society.

Gandhi was frequently jailed and beaten himself, over

a period of many years, but he and his followers continued to persist. Finally, in 1914, 20 years after Gandhi's struggle had begun, the South African government granted several new civil rights to Indians. Soon after, Gandhi returned to India and began an even more difficult struggle—the drive to free his homeland from the colonial grip of the British Empire.

After years of struggle with France for dominance over India, Britain had taken control of the vast nation in the mid-18th century. Despite repeated uprisings and revolts, the British had remained in power for more than 150 years and seemed destined to stay for 150 more. There seemed to be no way for the huge but impoverished population of India to defeat the mightiest empire in the history of the world. But there was a way, and the little man named Gandhi held the key: satyagraha.

Gandhi began working with ordinary workers, using the nonviolent techniques he had developed in South Africa in labor disputes with employers. He and his followers succeeded in winning concessions for textile workers, among others, but Gandhi was far from satisfied. From the beginning, he had a much more ambitious goal in mind. He wanted the British out of India. He wanted his people to be free to rule themselves.

Although Gandhi practiced nonviolence, many other

independence-hungry Indians did not. By 1919, the British Parliament was so alarmed by growing political violence in India that it passed the so-called Rowatt Bills, imposing heavy punishments for anti-British violence. Gandhi felt that the moment had come to launch direct nonviolent action against British rule. He called for national satyagraha on April 6. In addition to massive civil disobedience, a general strike shut down businesses all over the country.

Gandhi was arrested, but the satyagraha continued. The colonial authorities in the Punjab region were so frightened by a massive demonstration in Amritsar that they responded with incredible violence. Troops opened fire on a huge crowd, killing or wounding 1,600 people.

Shock and anger swept across the country. Many Indians reacted violently, but Gandhi responded by going on a three-day fast. He announced that he was paying penance for the loss of self-discipline on the part of his fellow Indians. For Gandhi, self-discipline was the heart of satyagraha: He knew that nonviolent action requires more self-control—and more courage—than violence does.

The next year, Gandhi called for massive noncooperation with the British. He asked all Indians to refuse to trade with British companies, go to the colonial schools run by the British, or even to appeal to the British-run courts.

India was a fractured nation. In addition to the great struggle between the British and the Indians for control of the enormous country, Indian society itself was torn by strife between Hindus and Muslims, caste and caste, rich and poor. Gandhi worked tirelessly to bridge the gulfs between all of the country's bitterly divided religious, ethnic, and social groups.

Gandhi had enormous personal courage. In South Africa, he had nursed plague victims most medical people were afraid to treat, and led a medical corps on to battlefields during the Boer and Zulu wars. Now, time after time, he went to prison, often combining his period in jail with long and dangerous fasts, drawing attention to his cause. His obvious goodness and greatness of spirit earned him the title of mahatma, which means both "wise man" and "great soul."

The willpower and bravery of the mahatma was matched by that of his followers. Again and again, masses of the Indian people showed their determination and willingness to suffer, in order to assert their human dignity and accomplish their goal of independence.

As an astonished journalist described one demonstration: "Suddenly, at a word of command, scores of native police rushed upon the advancing marchers and rained blows on their heads. . . . Not one of the marchers even raised an arm to fend off the blows. They went down like tenpins. From where I stood, I heard the sickening whacks of the clubs on unprotected skulls. . . . In two or three minutes the ground was quilted with bodies . . . the survivors without breaking ranks silently and doggedly marched on until struck down."[2]

Many Indians, impatient for violent action against the colonial rulers, could not understand this willingness to suffer without striking back. They saw nonviolence as a form of weakness. To them, Gandhi explained that "nonviolence does not mean meek submission to the will of the evildoer, but it means pitting of one's whole soul against the will of the tyrant. Working under the laws of our being, it is possible for a single individual to deny the whole might of an unjust empire to save his honor, his religion, his soul and lay the foundation for that empire's fall or its regeneration. And so I am not pleading for India to practice nonviolence because she is weak. I want her to practice nonviolence being conscious of her strength and power."[3]

Other revolutionary groups ignored Gandhi's advice, but through it all, Gandhi and his followers marched doggedly on toward the goal of independence. They rejected violence, even though others were slaughtering one another around them, and frequently attacking them as well. And ultimately, they succeeded where the others failed.

The details of the story of Indian independence are extremely complicated, but in 1947 the British announced that they would leave India the following year. Few doubted that the main credit for this went to Gandhi and satyagraha.

The end of British rule did not mean the end of strife for India, however. The huge colony was to be partitioned—or divided—into two independent countries, India and Pakistan. India would be primarily Hindu; Pakistan would be Muslim. Nonetheless, riots broke out between Hindu and Muslim mobs quarreling over who would control various parts of the region once the British left.

Gandhi was deeply grieved by the internal violence. Although he was nearly 80 years old and in poor health, he began another fast to encourage the groups to make peace with each other. He seemed to have succeeded when leaders from the various groups announced a truce. Less than two weeks later, on the way to his daily prayers, he was shot dead by a young Hindu who hated him for his efforts to reconcile with the Muslims.

Gandhi died—as he had lived—in the cause of peace and brotherhood. But, by his life, he had shown the enormous power of nonviolent civil disobedience to change the history of the world.

Noncooperation in Prison

The power of nonviolence was demonstrated on a much smaller scale by World War II-era conscientious objectors (COs) who used nonviolent tactics in the prisons and work camps to which they were sent for refusing to participate in the war. The pacifist prisoners carried out their own form of satyagraha: going on hunger strikes, refusing to do expected work, and generally disrupting prison routines to protest what they considered injustices.

In 1943, two COs protesting the Selective Service Act went on a total fast at the Danbury Correctional Institution in Connecticut. Worried that they might starve to death, prison officials tied them up and fed them through tubes. Even then, the prisoners refused to eat anything voluntarily for almost three months.[4] Their fast did nothing to change the federal draft law, but it served as a powerful witness to their beliefs. It also impressed other prisoners, showing them that they had some control over their lives even in their tiny cells.

Protests against racial segregation in the prisons were more directly effective. The pacifists considered segregation unjust, and many refused to cooperate with the prison system that enforced it. After a 135-day "strike" by 18 COs, Danbury integrated its dining hall. One frustrated warden of a western prison confessed to a prisoner that he yearned for "the good old days," when he had only "simple murderers and bank robbers for prisoners"![5]

They were so much easier to deal with. Many of the protesting COs would emerge from prison with a new awareness of the power of nonviolent protest. They would form the core of the civil rights demonstrators who would use similar nonviolent tactics in the civil rights movement that transformed American society in the decades after the war.

The Civil Rights Movement

Prisons weren't the only institutions that were segregated. Until the 1960s, virtually all institutions in the American South were segregated by law. Members of different races were not allowed to marry, go to the same schools, eat in the same restaurants, or even use the same public toilets. Although blacks and whites could ride in the same buses and attend the same movie theaters, they had to sit in different areas.

Southerners defended segregation by claiming that although the facilities were separate, they were equal. In reality, however, the facilities available to whites were much better than those allowed to blacks. What's more, African-

Americans who violated segregation laws were fined or jailed. Those who spoke out against them were often terrorized, threatened, beaten, tortured, and even killed.

The National Association for the Advancement of Colored People and other groups filed lawsuits to end this massive denial of civil rights. They won a monumental victory in 1954, when the U.S. Supreme Court ruled that segregation of public schools was unconstitutional. Separate schools, the Court ruled, were "inherently unequal." That ruling was followed by others striking down laws that segregated public beaches, golf courses, and other public places.[6]

But Southern officials clung to their segregation laws. Supported by most Southern whites, they refused to enforce the rulings of the Court. Unless the federal government was willing to occupy the Southern states militarily, it seemed that segregation would remain the reality there forever.

Then, on December 1, 1955, a black woman named Rosa Parks boarded a bus in Montgomery, Alabama. She took her seat in the black section in the rear of the bus and settled in for the ride. It was a busy day, however, and the white section quickly filled up. Not finding a place to sit in his own section of the bus, a white passenger demanded Parks's seat. Under the segregation laws, she was required to give it to him. But she was tired after a hard day's work and she refused, even after the bus driver ordered her to surrender her place. Outraged whites called the police and Rosa Parks was arrested.[7]

Black citizens in Montgomery decided that the time had come to overturn the laws segregating the city's transportation system. They launched a black boycott of the buses. The man chosen to lead the boycott was a young minister named Martin Luther King, Jr. As a college student, King had believed that the only way to "solve our problem of segregation was an armed revolt."[8] But now he called on the black people of Montgomery to fight the problem with "passive resistance and the weapon of love."[9]

King and others involved in the boycott were viciously harassed by angry whites. King was jailed twice. His family received scores of threatening phone calls. One night, the front of their house was blasted away by a bomb. But all the while, he and many other black citizens of Montgomery kept up their nonviolent protest.

The boycott organizers eventually won a court ruling desegregating Montgomery's buses, and with them the other public transportation systems of the South. By that time, the city officials were ready to give in. The buses were quickly integrated. It was the first of many nonviolent victories the civil rights movement would win during the next decade.

In February 1960, black college students sat down at the white lunch counter in a Greensboro, North Carolina, dime store and asked to be served. When the white waitresses refused to serve them, they simply stayed where they were, silently demanding their right to eat like anyone else. Although they were not served that day, they came back the next day. And the next. A new kind of protest had begun. News of the Greensboro "sit-ins" spread rapidly. Before long, young African-Americans, as well as a few white sympathizers, were sitting in at restaurants across the South.

Virtually all of the young people were cursed at and insulted. Many were arrested. Some had eggs or other food thrown at them, or were clubbed and beaten by angry whites. But for the most part, they endured the abuse with calm and patience.

The sit-ins had a telling effect. They touched the consciences of sensitive white people, who respected the courage and dignity of the young people, and the reasonableness of their demands. On another level, they made segregation uncomfortable for everyone: waitresses, storeowners, and customers alike. This meant they were bad for business. The combination of moral and economic pressure proved extremely effective. Three months after the first sit-in, ten dime stores in Nashville, Tennessee, integrated their lunch counters. For the first time in the modern South, white people and black people were eating together at the same lunch counters.[10]

Later that same year, groups of blacks and whites launched the first freedom rides, challenging the segregation of public transportation by traveling together by bus through the South. At one stop on their journey, they were attacked by a white mob, apparently with the approval of the police. Three of them were badly beaten, including a white representative of the U.S. Department of Justice.

Such violence against civil rights protestors was common. Over and over again, peaceful demonstrators were attacked by mobs, clubbed to the ground, or savaged by police dogs. Members of the Ku Klux Klan and other racist groups routinely assaulted civil rights workers, bombed their churches, and burned their homes and offices. And still the protestors persisted. From the time of Rosa Parks, through the sit-in and beyond, the hymn "We Shall Not Be Moved" was the anthem of the civil rights movement.

Many of those who took part in the nonviolent struggle were killed. Among others: Medgar Evers, the leader of the National Association for the Advancement of Colored People in Jackson, Mississippi, was killed outside his home in 1963; three young Northerners, two white and one black, were killed by a group of racists led by several policemen near Meridian, Mississippi, in 1964; Viola Liuzzo, a white woman from Detroit, was shot to death for giving a ride to black freedom marchers in Alabama in 1965; and Martin Luther King, Jr., himself was assassinated in Memphis, Tennessee, in 1968.

And still the movement as a whole refused to meet violence with violence. A few groups, like the Black Panthers and the Black Muslims, urged black people to defend themselves if attacked. But most—including King's own Southern Christian Leadership Conference (SCLC), the Student Nonviolent Coordinating Committee (SNCC), and the Congress of Racial Equality (CORE)—insisted on nonviolence and passive resistance.

Some of the civil rights demonstrators, like SNCC's leaders, believed in nonviolence primarily as a tactic. White segregationists in the South heavily outnumbered and outarmed those who believed in full civil rights for black people. If it came to a showdown, force against force, the African-Americans and their supporters were sure to lose. Besides, violence would frighten away many white people, Northern and Southern, who might otherwise support the cause of civil rights.

Others, like King, believed in nonviolence as a spiritual and religious force. King was a Christian minister. Asked where he came by his beliefs, he acknowledged that he had long been a student of Gandhi, although he traced the roots of his beliefs to a different source. "This business of passive resistance and nonviolence is the gospel of Jesus," King declared. "I went to Gandhi through Jesus."[11]

King believed that it was the black American's duty to show the white American the redeeming power of love and the willingness to suffer for what was morally right. The real struggle, he believed, was not between white and black, but between "justice and injustice."[12] The real goal was not the betterment of black Americans, but of all Americans. Over and over again, he appealed to African-Americans to refuse to hate. "Don't ever let anyone pull you so low as to hate them," he warned. "We must use the weapon of love. We must have compassion and understanding for those who hate us."[13]

The nonviolent civil rights movement accomplished a staggering transformation in American society. Before the day Rosa Parks got on that bus in Montgomery, African-Americans in the South were not only denied full use of public facilities, but also usually were forbidden to vote. In many parts of the country, they could not seek public office, they could not enroll in state universities, they could not even participate in sporting events with white athletes. Even in the North, there was no black player in major league baseball until Jackie Robinson was signed in 1945.

There is still a great deal of racism and discrimination in American society today. But it is nowhere near as extensive or as crippling as it was when it had the force of law. It is still harder for a typical black person to succeed in the wider society today than it is for a typical white—but not so long ago it was all but impossible.

Today, there is no longer any question among thinking Americans about the extent of African-Americans' abilities. Black lawyers practice alongside whites in major law firms, black doctors serve on the staffs of the best hospitals and clinics, and black teachers are prominent in the best schools. There are even black Supreme Court justices, neurosurgeons, and presidents of nonsegregated universities. What's more, their presence in these positions is not considered remarkable. None of this would have been possible without the brave peace commandos, black and white, who used nonviolence and passive resistance to end legal segregation a quarter century ago.

Chapter Six

Vietnam

One day in 1967, Martin Luther King, Jr., was leafing through the radical magazine *Ramparts* while eating at an airport restaurant. He came to a picture of a grieving Vietnamese mother holding her dead baby in her arms. The infant had been horribly burned by an American chemical weapon called napalm. King pushed aside his food. A friend asked if there was something wrong with it. "Nothing will ever taste any good for me," answered King, "until I do everything I can to end that war."[1] A great many other Americans felt the same way.

U.S. Involvement in Vietnam

Vietnam had been a French colony until the 1950s, when the French were driven out by a Communist-led revolution. An election was planned to choose a government for the newly independent Vietnam, but the process was blocked by the United States, which realized that the Communist leader Ho Chi Minh was bound to win. In order to prevent the Communists from gaining control of the whole country, the United States supported an international agreement that divided the former colony into two different countries: North Vietnam, governed by Ho Chi Minh and the Communists, and South Vietnam, led by an anti-Communist government allied with the United States.

The Vietnam War was a struggle between the South Vietnamese government and Communist Viet Cong rebels supported by the government in the North. From the start, the U.S. government sent military "advisers" to help the South. By the early 1960s, tens of thousands of Americans were in South Vietnam, no longer just "advising" but taking part in combat.

The U.S. government argued that if the South lost the war, the Communists would overrun not only Vietnam but all of Southeast Asia. For nearly a decade, this argument seemed to satisfy most of those Americans aware that the United States was involved in Vietnam at all. Most were not.

As late as 1962, a peace demonstration of hundreds of students in Washington, D.C., centered on nuclear disarmament and cold war issues. The growing U.S. involvement in the hot war in Vietnam was hardly mentioned, if at all. But when American casualties started mounting in the early 1960s, resistance to U.S. involvement began to grow. Few Americans wanted the dreaded Communists to make gains anywhere, but many found it hard to see why tens of thousands of young Americans had to be killed or maimed to stop them.

Before long, the Vietnam War would produce the biggest, broadest-based, and most active antiwar movement in U.S. history.

Early Opponents of the War

The huge antiwar movement that grew up in the 1960s was made up of several different elements. There were the traditional pacifists, of course, many of whom had already been active in the civil rights movement, where they had learned and practiced the tactics of nonviolence. But there were also more intensely political groups like the Students for a Democratic Society (SDS), which belonged to what was called the New Left and saw the United States as taking over France's old role of colonial master in Vietnam. They dreamed of overturning the American economic and social systems as well as of ending the war in Vietnam.

Still another major branch of the antiwar movement came from among the hippies. These were the "flower children," who, in the words of a Harvard psychology professor named Timothy Leary, had "tuned in, turned on, and dropped out." They had "tuned in" to their own needs and desires, "turned on" to drugs like marijuana and LSD to help them explore the boundaries of human experience, and "dropped out" of what they saw as a materialistic and rules-bound culture. Trying to practice total personal freedom, many of them lived together in communes, sharing their possessions and their emotions more or less casually.

Like the more traditional pacifists, the hippies were nonviolent. They talked of the power of love to overcome the power of the military's guns. Allison Krause was not known as a hippie, but when she put that flower in the barrel of the guardsman's gun, she was making a hippie-style gesture.

Many of the revolutionaries, on the other hand, pressured the movement toward more disruptive and violent activities. One outlaw group called the Weathermen moved toward terrorism, setting off bombs in public places. On the University of Wisconsin campus, two antiwar activists blew up a portion of a campus building where research was being done for the Defense Department. A graduate student was killed in the explosion. For the most part, however, the antiwar demonstrations stayed peaceful, except when police, prowar demonstrators, or outraged veterans attacked the protestors.

Although most veterans seemed to support the war, some did not. As the war dragged on, a new element was added to the peace movement in the form of a minority of returning veterans. Bitterly disillusioned by what they had seen of the war firsthand, these veterans formed Vietnam Veterans against the War and joined the student protestors.

Antiwar Activities and the Colleges

Antiwar feeling tended to flow outward from the college campuses. It was in the universities that people had the most time to spend studying history, morality, and politics, and thinking about big issues like war and peace. It was there that large numbers of young people had the energy and the freedom to mount demonstrations and protests. And, most of all, it was there that many of the same people faced the prospect of being drafted and sent to fight in Vietnam. Political and moral concerns, combined with intensely personal worries about the future, led many students to take a stand against the war.

Some faculty members and college administrators resented the antiwar activity on campus. They considered it a distraction from the real business of the university. Others encouraged the protesting students. Some held "teach-ins," interrupting their classes for a day or two to discuss the war.

Early Demonstrations against the War

The first nationwide protest against the war was held in December 1964. Two months later, 14 antiwar protestors were arrested for blocking the entrance to the UN building in New York City. In April, 15,000 protestors showed up in front of the White House. Antiwar sit-ins blocked the New York Armed Forces Day parade in May, while 17,000 people came to an antiwar rally at Madison Square Garden in June.

By then, opposition to the war had spread far afield from the college campuses. Martin Luther King, Jr., had publicly declared his opposition to the war, and so had Dr. Benjamin Spock, the pediatrician whose best-selling book on child rearing had influenced many of the parents of the young men and women serving in Vietnam, as well as the parents of many of the protesting students. The protestors also included two famous pacifists who had been in the forefront of antiwar activities for many decades. Both Dorothy Day and Jeannette Rankin led demonstrations against the war.

At one big demonstration in Washington, D.C., late in November 1965, observers counted as many middle-aged adults as students.[2] An antiwar march in New York City drew 20,000 people in the spring of 1966. In October 1967, 50,000 antiwar demonstrators marched from the Lincoln Memorial to the Pentagon in Washington.

Other Forms of Protest

Mass rallies and demonstrations like those mentioned above were the most visible forms of protest, but there were many others. Demonstrators sat in at draft centers and campus recruiting centers around the country, disrupting normal activities until the police arrested them or drove them away.

Following the example set by Henry David Thoreau more than a century before, thousands of Americans refused to pay all or part of their taxes. They wrote to the Internal Revenue Service declaring their refusal to pay for an unjust war.

In Baltimore, Maryland, several protestors, including Daniel and Philip Berrigan, two brothers who were Roman Catholic priests, poured duck blood over the files of the Baltimore Selective Service office. Four were captured and sentenced to several years in jail.

Horrifyingly, two protestors—one a Quaker and one a Catholic pacifist—set themselves on fire to protest the war. They were following the lead of several Buddhist monks in Vietnam itself who had chosen this way to demonstrate the horrors of the war and to express their desire for peace.

Daniel Ellsberg, an antiwar intellectual who had worked for the State Department, found his own unique way to fight against the war. He gave a top secret government study revealing government lies and misrepresentations about the war to the *New York Times* to print. The study, published as the "Pentagon Papers," caused many people to reexamine their support for the war. Ellsberg was arrested and charged with espionage and other major crimes. A true peace commando if ever there was one, Ellsberg might have gone to prison for life if the charges hadn't been thrown out when it was revealed that the government had committed many misdeeds in trying to collect evidence against him.

Bringing Down a President

The more opposition to the war grew back home, the more America's involvement in Vietnam seemed to grow. By the end of 1965, there had been nearly 150,000 American servicemen and servicewomen in Southeast Asia; a year later, there were 389,000.[3] The supposed "civil war" in Vietnam was becoming an American war. In some weeks, more Americans were being killed than Vietnamese.

Although many prominent Americans had spoken out against the war by 1967, few "respectable" politicians dared to come out against the war. One exception was Eugene McCarthy, a Democratic senator from Minnesota. McCarthy not only expressed his disagreement with the war, but challenged the Democratic president, Lyndon B. Johnson, who was conducting it. McCarthy declared himself a candidate for the Democratic presidential nomination.

Most political experts scoffed at McCarthy's chances. It was almost impossible to take the nomination from a sitting president. But in the first presidential primary in New Hampshire, McCarthy got 40 percent of the vote—and that was in a conservative, presumably prowar state!

The experts hadn't reckoned on the effect of the antiwar movement. Thousands of antiwar activists had volunteered to work for the maverick senator. Not wanting to annoy conservative voters, they had gotten "clean for Gene." They'd cut their long hair short, doffed their colorful hippie costumes in favor of ordinary clothes, and gone door-to-door around the state campaigning for the senator.

President Johnson was a shrewd politician. He knew that he might lose the nomination because of the growing opposition to the war. Even if he won it, the fight with his fellow Democrats would be so damaging that he would probably lose the election to the Republican candidate in the fall. Facing these realities, he announced that he would not run for reelection. Johnson's vice president, Hubert Humphrey, who also supported the war, became a candidate for the Democratic nomination. So did Robert Kennedy, who opposed the war despite being the brother of slain president John F. Kennedy who had sent the first U.S. troops there.

As the primaries went on, the antiwar candidates, McCarthy and Kennedy, got the majority of the votes between them. It seemed more and more likely that the Democrats would nominate a peace candidate at their convention in Chicago. Depending how you looked at it, the antiwar movement—or the war itself—had brought down a president. It only remained to see if the war's opponents could elect a president who would end the war.

But then the peace movement was dealt a volley of devastating blows. Martin Luther King, Jr., was assassinated in April 1968, and Robert Kennedy was assassinated in Los Angeles in June of the same year—on the very day he won the California primary, the biggest primary of them all.

It soon became clear that when the Democrats met in Chicago they would nominate the prowar candidate Humphrey, after all. Thousands of antiwar demonstrators announced that they would go to Chicago to protest. The city was like an armed camp when they arrived. The National Guard had been called out to put down any possible trouble.

Chicago police watched warily as thousands of antiwar demonstrators gathered in Grant Park, where they camped out on the grass. Then, when they tried to march from the park to the convention center a few miles away, the police moved in with clubs and tear gas. In what was described by observers as a "police riot," they attacked the demonstrators fiercely, wounding at least 100 of them. For good measure, they attacked several newsmen and cameramen and members of the press as well, whom they accused of supporting the protestors.

Inside the convention hall, an antiwar delegate appealed to city authorities to "end the police state of terror,"[4] but the attack went on until the police got tired of it. The next day, police raided the offices of Senator McCarthy, the defeated peace candidate.

Eight of the activists who had come to Chicago to protest were charged with conspiracy to incite a riot. The defendants represented several different branches of the antiwar movement. Abbie Hoffman and Jerry Rubin, for example, were leaders of a freewheeling group of hippielike pranksters who called themselves Yippies. Dave Dellinger, on the other hand, was a serious-minded pacifist who often wore a suit and tie, and who believed in "the revolutionary potential of nonviolence."[5] Tom Hayden and Rennie Davis were New Left leaders of the Students for a Democratic Society. Bobby Seale was one of the founders of the Black Panthers. And so on.

The defendants did their best to turn their trial into a public debate on the Vietnam War. Seale tried to represent himself, but his flamboyantly combative manner of doing so angered the judge. At one point, the judge had him chained and gagged in the courtroom. Eventually, his trial was separated from that of the other defendants.

In the end, two of the Chicago Seven (as the remaining defendants were known) were acquitted. The rest were found guilty of less serious charges. Even their lawyers, who had encouraged them in their disruptive behavior during the trials, were found guilty of contempt of court. The convictions were later overturned by an appeals court because of the mistakes and obvious prejudice of the trial judge.

The Biggest Protests of them All

The election of 1968 was fought between Hubert H. Humphrey, the prowar Democrat, and the Republican candidate, Richard M. Nixon. Nixon also supported the war but claimed to have a plan to bring it to a successful end, although he wouldn't say what the plan was. Nixon won.

Nixon didn't end the war, but he tried to "Vietnamize" it, to force the South Vietnamese to take on responsibility for actually fighting the war, allowing most American troops to return home. Within a few months of his taking office, the number of American troops in Vietnam peaked at more than 500,000, after which he began to withdraw them slowly, turning over more and more of the ground fighting to the South Vietnamese army. But at the same time, he expanded the American bombing. Meanwhile, aware of the growing antiwar sentiment in the country, Congress began limiting the president's authority to spread the war into Vietnam's neighbors.

And, all the while, protests were growing larger and increasingly tense in the United States. National Guardsmen attacked 1,500 students blocking the entrances to campus buildings at the University of Wisconsin. Smaller groups were driven from buildings at Columbia University and elsewhere.

The biggest antiwar demonstrations of all took place in the fall of 1969. Millions of people took part in a nationwide moratorium—a kind of ministrike—on October 15. All over the country, people found their own ways to protest: by not going to work or school, by conducting "teach-ins," or just by wearing black armbands. A month later, 250,000 people crammed into the vast mall in front of the Washington Monument in Washington, D.C.

The next spring brought the tragedy at Kent State. After that, both the war and the protests seemed to be winding down. Ten thousand marchers gathered in Washington in the summer of 1971, around the same time that American Vietnam casualties set five-year lows.

But still the war dragged on. South Vietnamese deaths were nearing 200,000. North Vietnamese and Viet Cong deaths were approaching one million. And, however slowly, the numbers of American casualties continued to mount, with deaths climbing over 50,000 and injuries over 300,000.[6]

To the antiwar activists, the new deaths seemed even

more pointless—and terrible—than the earlier ones. Everyone knew the war was ending and the United States was pulling out. Why did the killings still go on? "Just before the end," sang an exasperated folksinger named Phil Ochs, "even treason might be worth a try."[7]

The Effect of the Protests

By early 1973, the last American troops were finally gone from Vietnam. The war was over.

The protestors greeted the end of the war with celebration. They believed that they had won. Their long efforts had finally produced peace. Those who believed that the United States had been on the wrong side from the beginning were particularly glad that the war had ended without a U.S.–South Vietnamese victory. Others cared nothing about that. For them, there were no victors in any war, only the dead and the maimed and the orphaned.

On the other hand, many prowar Americans bitterly blamed the protestors for "losing" the war. They claimed that the protests had hurt the morale of the military. What's more, by turning public opinion against the war, they had led Congress and two presidents to tie the military's hands, so that the United States could not win. When the Communists took control of all Vietnam in 1975, many angry Americans blamed the "peaceniks."

Despite the claims on both sides, there is no way to tell how much effect the Vietnam protests actually had. Despite the massive demonstrations and the many acts of personal defiance, the Vietnam War was still the longest war in U.S. history. Critics charged that the protestors had made a lot of noise, but had done little to change American policy. It had been only the reality of more than 50,000 young Americans coming home in body bags that had done that.

For whatever reasons, the majority of the American public had started out supporting the war in Vietnam and ended up wanting the United States to leave. In a sense, the antiwar movement had won the battle for public opinion. But, even while most people came around to agree with the movement's main point—that the United States should get out of Vietnam—they never accepted the movement itself. To the end, many Americans regarded the antiwar protestors as unpatriotic. Many still do. Some of those who took a stand against the war are still paying a price today. Even President Bill Clinton still suffers criticism for the anti-Vietnam stand he took as a college student.

In any case, the antiwar protestors had taken their

stand. Many were content to know that the war was over, and that they had done what they could to end it. Most of all, they felt, they had been on the right side—the side of peace.

They may not have ended the Vietnam War, but they had "washed their hands" of it, as Thoreau had done with the Mexican War more than a century before.

Chapter Seven

"Suppose They Gave a War and Nobody Came?"

On October 15, 1965, in the middle of the Vietnam War, a tall young man with blond hair stepped forward during a demonstration in front of an army induction center in New York City. His name was David Miller, and he was holding a draft card: a small card that all young men were required to carry at all times to prove that they had registered for the draft. Then, with a crowd and cameras looking on, he burned the card.

Under the draft laws of the time, that act was a serious crime. The card burning was a symbol that everyone could understand of Miller's refusal to cooperate with the draft, or with the war, in any way. By burning the card publicly, he was not so much defying the legal authorities as declaring that he would accept personal and legal responsibility for his act. If society wished to punish him, it could do so. This willingness to take

123

the consequences of his act was an important part of the philosophy of civil disobedience put forth by Thoreau, Gandhi, and King.

Miller's defiant protest sparked draft card burnings by thousands of other protestors all over the country. One result, as Thoreau had predicted, was a "clogging" of the enforcement system. Of 110,000 people who burned their draft cards,[1] only a fraction ever went to jail.

Noncooperation is the heart of any effective antiwar movement. And the heart of noncooperation is draft resistance.

Wars are fought by people. This is a simple fact, but one that is sometimes easy to forget. We speak of armies attacking other armies, bombers annihilating cities, ground-to-air missiles destroying incoming planes, and so on. But behind all these weapons there are human beings. Once, it was knights with swords, bowmen with longbows, and peasant soldiers with pikes. Later, it was cavalrymen with sabers and guns, and infantrymen with rifles and bayonets. Today, it may be fighter pilots, and technicians at nuclear missile sites. But, no matter how sophisticated the weapons, it still takes human beings to operate them.

In 1914, the great scientist Albert Einstein urged his colleagues "to refuse to cooperate in research for war purposes." In addition, he praised young men who refused to join the military as "pioneers of a warless world," and advised the newspapers "to encourage [their] readers to refuse war service."[2] Einstein recognized that war would be impossible without the cooperation of the individual human beings who build and operate the weapons of war on both sides. It is extremely ironic that it would be Einstein's own theories that would make it possible for others to develop nuclear explosives, the most terrible of all weapons of war.

"He's the universal soldier," sang the folksinger Buffy St. Marie, "and he really is to blame. Without him all this killing can't go on."[3]

Draft Avoiders, Dodgers, and Resisters

Some wars are fought by volunteers. This has been true of the wars the United States has been involved in during the past two decades. There has been no draft since 1973, because the military conflicts the U.S. has been involved in since Vietnam have been relatively small and brief, and the government has had no trouble finding volunteers. Since the early 1980s, however, young men have been required to register with the Selective Service office, in case the government wishes to reactivate the draft, which it can do at any time.

When the draft is in effect, young men are plucked out of the population and ordered to fight, whether they want to or not. But, what if they refuse? "Suppose they gave a war and nobody came?" suggested a peace slogan at the time of the Vietnam War. It's a powerful question.

People wishing to decline their invitations to a war do so in three different ways: by avoiding the draft, by dodging it, or by resisting it. *Draft avoiders* find legal ways to escape military service, usually by getting a selective service classification that makes them ineligible for military service, either temporarily or permanently. They break no law because they are never actually drafted and therefore are not legally required to serve.

Draft dodgers or *evaders* escape military service in ways that are fraudulent or illegal. Either they avoid being drafted by faking medical conditions that would make them ineligible for service, or they are drafted and then flee by going underground, or escaping to a foreign country, as some 68,000 young men did during Vietnam.[4] Draft evasion is a crime. It can be punished by imprisonment or a fine. In general, the draft laws have been enforced more strictly and punishments have been more harsh in wartime than in peacetime.

Draft resisters also violate the law, but they do so openly. Some even do so publicly, burning their draft cards or writing letters to their local papers declaring their unwillingness to serve.

Are Draft Dodgers Peace Commandos?

It can be argued that only draft resisters deserve to be called peace commandos. Draft avoiders take no risks, while draft evaders take no public stand and try to escape any punishment for their refusal to participate in the military. They do not so much try to end war as to escape it, and where is the honor—or even the usefulness—of that?

However, a case can be made that draft dodgers as well as draft resisters should be considered peace commandos. In a sense, everyone drafted to serve in the military is drafted in the fight for peace as well. He (and soon, perhaps, she) is faced with a stark choice—a choice that he can no longer avoid making. Will he side with war or peace? Violence or nonviolence? Will what he does help the military machine or hinder it? Will he become a "universal soldier," or a commando for peace?

A soldier is a soldier, whether he wants to be in uniform or not, and whether he or she sees action in combat or not. A draftee who disobeys the order to join the military is at legal risk whether he wants to be or not, and whether he is caught and punished or not.

A draft dodger who escapes military service through fraud or deceit is certainly less honorable than a resister who burns his draft card in front of an army induction center; just as a soldier who does paperwork in the United States is less heroic than one who single-handedly takes a disputed hill from a strong enemy force. But a draftee doesn't have to be a hero to be recognized as a soldier, and he doesn't have to go to jail to be a peace commando.

For, as Thoreau understood a century and a half ago, it is not necessary for individuals to devote themselves to the eradication of evil, but it is a person's duty to refuse to become a part of it. In that very limited sense, anyone who refuses to participate in a war in which he or she doesn't believe is fulfilling that duty.

The First Drafts

During the War of 1812, President Madison asked Congress to draft 40,000 men into the army. Congress passed conscription bills to do this, but the war ended before the draft began.[5] The first large-scale conscriptions came during the Civil War, when both sides drafted men to fight.

In the North, almost all men between the ages of 20 and 45 were eligible, except for high public officials, men with families to support, and members of the clergy. Individuals could legally buy their way out of the draft, however, by paying $300 or finding someone else to serve for them. In the South, men between 18 and 35 were eligible. Later, the upper limit was raised to 45. Southern men, too, could avoid service by hiring someone to fight in their place. Women didn't serve in the military at all, so they were not eligible to be drafted.

The Civil War draft probably encouraged more people to enlist than were actually drafted. This was particularly true in the North, where geographical areas were given quotas to fulfill. As long as enough people enlisted in that area, the draft never actually went into force. Many places escaped the draft altogether.

Poor working-class men on both sides of the war were outraged that the wealthy could buy their way out. In the North, there were draft riots in many big cities. One of the worst took place in New York City in July 1863. Mobs made up mostly of Irish-Americans went on a rampage. They burned government buildings to the ground and trashed the homes of wealthier city residents. Not content with taking out their rage on the government and the wealthy, they attacked poor black people as well. The Irish-Americans and the African-Americans were together at the very bottom of the economic labor in the North. They competed bitterly for the very worst jobs society had to provide. The rioters, who hated the African-Americans to begin with, now hated them even more because they blamed antislavery feeling for the war. They killed scores of their black neighbors and burned down an orphanage for African-American children.

The riot, which went on for four days, was so violent that the police were helpless. Army troops had to be called back from the battlefields. Even then, peace wasn't restored until after a pitched battle between the rioters on one side and the troops, police, militia, and West Point cadets on the other. More than 100 people were killed, most of them Irish-American rioters and their African-American victims. Somewhere between 300 and 900 others on both sides were injured. The conscription law was eventually changed to keep the rich from buying their way out.

Conscientious Objectors

The Civil War draft rioters were not pacifists. Although many of them sympathized with the South, they were not really protesting the war. They just didn't want to serve in it. If they were protesting anything, it was the unfairness of letting the wealthy escape the draft while the poor could not.

But there were also legitimate pacifists who opposed the conscription measures on both sides. As always, pious members of the peace churches were determined not to serve, draft or no draft. They appealed to the authorities to excuse them on conscientious grounds. The North and the South treated them differently. The South excused them from the war at first, but forced them into service later when Confederate manpower ran low. The North made no special exceptions for them in the beginning. But when the conscription law was changed in the wake of the draft riots, those who objected to military service on religious grounds were allowed to buy their way out of the draft even when others could not. What's more, those who were drafted were not forced to bear arms. They were allowed to perform alternative, nonviolent duties instead. From that time on, whenever there has been an active draft, the laws have made some provision for conscientious objectors.

What It Means to Be a Conscientious Objector

Conscientious objectors fall into several different categories. Like other peace commandos, some oppose all wars, while some oppose only those wars they see as unjust. Official government policy has traditionally insisted that only those who object to war itself, under any circumstances, can be classified as legal conscientious objectors and excused from fighting.

Despite this policy, many young men who morally object to particular wars consider themselves true conscientious objectors, and refuse to serve. They agree with the young Bill Clinton, who wrote that "no government . . . should have the power to make its citizens fight and die in a war they may oppose, a war which even possibly may be wrong, a war which, in any case, does not involve immediately the peace and freedom of the nation."[6]

One group of conscientious objectors refuses to fight but is willing to accept an obligation to serve with the military in nonviolent, noncombatant roles. Noncombatant doesn't mean safe from combat, however. Many world war and Vietnam COs served as medics, going into the battlefields to rescue wounded soldiers.

Other conscientious objectors refuse to serve in *any*

132

military role but are willing to do civilian work that contributes to "the national interest" instead. In practice, this has meant anything from physical labor on a conservation project to serving as an orderly in a mental institution, or even volunteering as a guinea pig in a medical experiment.

Still others flatly refuse to do any service at all. Today, when there is no actual draft, many will not even register with the Selective Service. They believe that it is wrong to cooperate in any way with the "war machine" and that registration is a form of cooperation. What's more, they argue, even the civilian jobs given to conscientious objectors in wartime help the war effort by freeing up other people to fight in their place.

Conscientious Objectors and the Law

Some noncooperators argue that they are protected by the Thirteenth Amendment to the U.S. Constitution, which forbids "involuntary servitude," but the courts have rejected this claim. Legally, CO status is granted under the First Amendment right to freedom of religion. During World War I, only members of recognized peace churches were accepted as conscientious objectors. During World War II, the standards were loosened when the Supreme Court ruled that anyone opposed to all war by reason "of religious training or belief" was eligible for CO status.

During the Vietnam War, local draft boards were pretty much allowed to set their own standards for who would or would not be awarded CO status. Some draft boards, whose members had their own doubts about the war, gave CO classifications to all who asked for it, whatever their religious beliefs. Others rarely granted CO status to anyone who did not belong to an established pacifist religion.

The Supreme Court has made several rulings concerning conscientious objectors. One holds that a conscientious objector can have a sincerely "religious" objection to war even if he does not believe in God; another, that a person does not have to object to all forms of violence, including self-defense, in order to qualify as a CO. The Court always maintained, however, that CO status should not be given to those who object only to some wars and not to others.[7]

Those Who Wouldn't Go

During World War I, draft-age men became subject to military law as soon as they got a notice in the mail ordering them to report for induction into the military. This was unfortunate for those who would not serve, because military law was much harsher than civilian law would have been. Four hundred and forty-six World War I conscientious objectors were court-martialed and sent to military prisons.[8] There, they were considered either cowards or traitors by many of the guards and fellow prisoners alike, and frequently mistreated. Because of the heavy punishments under military law, 142 men convicted of draft offenses were given life sentences. Seventeen were sentenced to death. None were ever actually executed, however, and even those with life sentences were eventually released.[9]

Some 4,750 other men were convicted of draft violations in civilian courts. No one knows how many were conscientious objectors, but most were probably not. Some opposed American participation in the war for political reasons. Some sympathized with Germany. Socialists and anarchists believed that the war was a quarrel between imperialist nations, in which the poor were forced to fight and die to protect the wealth of rich industrialists. Others tried to evade the draft for personal reasons. Many were terrified of warfare. Others hated the regimentation of military life or couldn't bear to leave their families.

The evaders tried a variety of ways to escape service.

Some faked physical or mental illness so the military wouldn't want them. Others took more extreme measures, mutilating themselves by shooting themselves in the foot or cutting off fingers. Many went into hiding.

Draft evasion of all kinds was especially common where large numbers of German-American immigrants and their descendants lived. In rural Wisconsin, one young man put on a dress and worked his family's fields masquerading as a woman throughout the war. Neighbors, most of whom were German-Americans themselves, often sympathized and helped the evaders hide from the authorities. Like the draft rioters of the Civil War, most of these evaders were not pacifists. They simply didn't want to fight their relatives.

Others refused to serve out of conscience. In 1915, Jessie Wallace Hughan and others formed the Anti-Enlistment League to encourage young men to resist the draft and oppose American entry into the war. At that time, only those who belonged to the recognized peace churches were accepted as conscientious objectors. Resisters who belonged to other religions or who opposed war or violence for nonreligious reasons were considered draft dodgers.

By World War II, only men who had already been inducted were subject to military law. This meant that most of the conscientious objectors accused of violating the draft laws were tried in civilian court. More than 6,086 conscientious objectors were sent to federal prison, compared with more than 30,000 who were granted CO status and excused from military service. Many of the COs performed alternative service of some kind. About 4,000 of those jailed were Jehovah's Witnesses who claimed status as ministers but were turned down; 157 were Black Muslims who refused to serve primarily because the military was segregated.[10]

Relatively few people were jailed for draft evasion during the Korean War, probably no more than 100 or 200 a year. But during the Vietnam War, the numbers of draft offenses of all kinds soared. Estimates of the number of draftees who refused to serve at all—whether by going to jail, going underground, or fleeing to a foreign country—range as high as 28,500.[11] Among them was the heavyweight boxing champion Muhammad Ali. Ali asked to be excused from service as a Black Muslim minister, but his local draft board turned down his request. Because he refused to serve in the military, Ali was stripped of his heavyweight title and sentenced to five years in jail and a $10,000 fine.

At least 450,000 of the men who actually entered the military deserted during the war.[12] Although many draft dodgers, resisters, and deserters went to jail, thousands of others did not. Even many of those who resisted publicly were never punished, thanks to a massive backlog of cases that clogged the legal system, just as Thoreau had suggested over a century earlier. The great majority of them received a presidential amnesty after the U.S. withdrew from the war.

Selective Service Registration Today

There has been no active draft in the United States for more than two decades, but young men are still required to register with the Selective Service when they turn 18. This is so the Selective Service will be able to find them easily, if and when the draft is reinstated.

In the days when men were actually being drafted—particularly when American troops were fighting somewhere in the world—registering for the draft was a monumental event. It meant the possibility that you could be snatched from your ordinary life and sent to fight, and perhaps to kill or die, whenever the government chose to call you. Today, many young people hardly think twice about registering. Some take it less seriously than applying for a driver's license.

A few committed pacifists still refuse to register, however. They believe that registering means accepting not only the *possibility* of serving in the armed forces, but also the *duty* to serve if called. Since they have no intention of serving, they will not sign up. Taking this stand means breaking the law and opening themselves up to some real penalties.

Under the 1982 Solomon Amendment, those who have not registered are not eligible for federally guaranteed student loans, Pell grants for education, or government job training programs. Under the Thurmond Amendment of 1985, those who have not registered cannot get jobs with the U.S. government, including the postal service.

If actually tried and convicted of refusing to register, resisters could be fined up to $250,000 and sentenced to five years in federal prison. Actual criminal prosecutions have been rare in recent years, although they would probably increase dramatically if the country got involved in an extended war.

There is no way to register as a conscientious objector. Nothing on today's Selective Service form allows you to claim any particular draft status. Since there is no draft, there is no effort to classify those who register. According to a spokesperson for the Selective Service System, the time for a conscientious objector to declare himself is after the draft is reinstated and you receive a notice to report for induction into the military.[13]

To people who work in draft resistance, this seems

terribly late in the process. No one knows what the details of the draft law will be if and when the draft is reinstated. Antiwar groups like the War Resisters League advise pacifists who choose to register to clearly indicate their opposition to war and military service somewhere on the form.[14]

The Respect of a President

Many people suspect the motives of young men who claim to be conscientious objectors in time of war. They consider them weaklings who hide behind moral beliefs to explain their cowardice. Others know better. They understand, as Gandhi did, that it can take as much courage to refuse to fight as it does to fight.

Among those who understood was President John Kennedy. Although he had served valiantly himself in World War II and was considered to be a militaristic president by many, Kennedy respected conscientious objectors. What's more, he recognized them as beacons of hope for the future. "War," Kennedy once said, "will exist until the distant day when the conscientious objector enjoys the same reputation and prestige the warrior does today."[15]

Chapter Eight

"Swords Into Plowshares"

I f everybody wants peace, and nobody wants war, why aren't more people pacifists?

The main reason seems to be fear.

We are used to solving international problems by military force. We understand that kind of force. In a sad sort of way, we're comfortable with it. And, as a nation, we are very good at it. America has been one of the world's great military powers for a long, long time. Today, we are unquestionably the strongest. We have more and better weapons—by far—than any other country in the world. When it comes to solving problems by military force, we have a tremendous advantage. Most of us are afraid to give up that advantage.

Pacifism seems dangerous. And it is. As Coleman McCarthy, the founder of the Center for Teaching Peace, has said: "Nonviolence is a risky philosophy to live by. It's no guarantee of safety."[1]

But violence is no guarantee of safety either. Just the opposite. More than a million people were killed in the Vietnam War, and millions more wounded. Were they safe? There were roughly 37,500,000 casualties (killed or wounded) in World War I. Were they safe?

Were the risks of trying to deal with the problems that caused those wars nonviolently really greater than the risks that killed those tens of millions of people?

But sometimes, say the militarists, you have to fight. Some villains are so terrible that you have to go to war to stop them. The Nazis slaughtered between 9 and 10 million innocent people. Surely they had to be stopped. But more than 50 million people died in the war that was fought to stop them. Was slaughtering 50 million people the only way to stop the slaughter of 10 million others? Was it really the *safest* way?

The pacifists say no.

They believe the world must find other ways to solve its problems.

The Peace Movement Today

Most American military actions since Vietnam have been relatively short-lived. Although some people have publicly opposed every military conflict the United States has entered, the invasions of Grenada and Panama, and even the war against Iraq, left little time for the forces of peace to mobilize against them. For this and other reasons, the modern peace movement has concentrated less on opposing particular military actions than on more long-range efforts.

Antinuclear groups like SANE and Physicians for Social Responsibility continue to lobby for an end to the stockpiling of nuclear weapons. Resistance groups like the War Resisters League and the Central Committee for Conscientious Objectors continue to counsel young men who refuse to register with Selective Service. The Fellowship of Reconciliation, the Catholic Peace Fellowship, and many other organizations continue to urge people in all walks of life to find nonviolent ways to deal with problems, in their personal lives as well as in international affairs.

What's more, there is a growing effort to introduce peace studies into the educational system. A number of high schools, colleges, and universities have introduced courses designed to promote peaceful ways of resolving conflicts.

In one of the most sweeping of such programs, each of Chicago's public secondary schools requires all students to take a course in conflict resolution at some point in their high-school careers.[2]

Encouraging Signs

The peace commandos have seen some encouraging signs lately. In 1989, the mighty Soviet Union collapsed and the Iron Curtain came crashing down without widespread war or bloodshed. This seems to mean that the cold war—which held the threat of nuclear annihilation over the world since the end of World War II—is over.

The end of the cold war has brought the possibility of a "peace dividend," the opportunity for resources to be taken out of the production of weapons and transferred to other purposes. It may at last be economically possible to provide for the basic needs of all Americans, with money that we have been spending on nuclear and other weapons of mass destruction. So far, the United States has been slow—and even reluctant—to stop expending massive amounts of its resources on weapons; but the possibility is there, and being considered.

Almost as heartening is the fact that democracy seems to be spreading peaceful roots in at least some of the nations of Eastern Europe. Some even chose peace commandos—like Vaclav Havel and Lech Walesa—to lead their governments in the months after the Iron Curtain's collapse.

Discouraging Signs

On the other hand, a massive "peaceable revolution" in China was put down with brutal force. And even in Eastern Europe, not all the changes have been bloodless. A large number of people were killed in Romania, including the dictator Nicolae Ceauçescu and his wife.

In the years after the Soviet Union's collapse, ethnic violence has broken out in many nations of Eastern Europe. In what used to be Yugoslavia, the violence has reached the level of a full-scale war, with large numbers of noncombatants being slaughtered solely because of their heritage or religion. And there are roughly 40 other military conflicts raging around the world as well.

What's more, the "peace dividend" has not been spent. Instead, we are producing and spending as much as ever on the weapons of war, even though the "need" for them seems to be greatly reduced.

For all the hopeful signs, then, there is still much work for the peace commandos to do.

The Peace Agenda for the Future

Demilitarization. It is not just the United States, but the world, that has become used to solving problems by military force. Pacifists in many countries are working to reduce their nations' reliance on military force. In this struggle to demilitarize the world, the United States is still the most important battlefield. With the disintegration of the Soviet Union, the United States is unquestionably the mightiest military power in the world. Just as importantly, it is the world's biggest supplier of weapons to other countries. American arms manufacturers supply more guns, bombs, and warplanes to other nations than all the rest of the arms suppliers in the world put together—a massive trade that is encouraged by the American government.[3]

Nuclear Arms Control. From the bombing of Hiroshima to the collapse of the Soviet Union, nuclear disarmament was the overriding concern of the peace movement. Since then, the threat of a world-destroying nuclear war between the United States and what was once the Soviet Union has faded, and concern about nuclear weapons has faded, too. But tens of thousands of nuclear warheads still exist. The main issue now is not heading off an intercontinental nuclear war, but halting the proliferation of nuclear weapons to new countries. The more nations that have them, the more likely they are to be used.

Education for Nonviolence. Any effort to demilitarize the world begins with demilitarizing the minds and hearts of individual people. Pacifists believe that nations' reliance on military force is a reflection of individual people's reliance on violence in their own lives. In both cases, they say, violence shows a failure of imagination. We rely on brute force because we can't think of any other way to solve our problems. The most basic step in the effort to reduce violence in the world is to teach people other methods of problem solving: ranging from negotiation, compromise, and persuasion to resistance, noncooperation, and civil disobedience.

Working for Social and Economic Justice. Wars don't just happen. They are caused by a variety of social, economic, and psychological evils: inequality, poverty, ethnic hatred, envy, greed, injustice, and many others. Pacifists have long known that it is impossible to combat war without combatting the causes of war as well. "If you want peace," states a pacifist slogan echoing Lucretia Mott, "work for justice." That is still the biggest challenge facing the peace commandos of the future.

Source Notes

Allison Krause

1. Erich Segal, "Death Story," *Ladies Home Journal,* October 1970, p. 101.

Chapter One

1. On the "Rush Limbaugh" syndicated radio program, April 6, 1993.
2. It is hard to get an exact count. Forty was the number cited by Congressman Alcee Hastings at hearings of the House Foreign Affairs Subcommittee on Europe on May 3, 1993. Others put the number even higher.
3. Ellen C. Collier, ed., *Instances of Use of United States Armed Forces Abroad, 1798–1983* (Washington, D.C.: Congressional Research Service, Library of Congress, 1983).
4. Joseph M. Kitagawa, "The Eightfold Path to Nirvana," *Great Religions of the World* (Washington, D.C.: National Geographic Society, 1971), p. 97.
5. Matt. 5:39.
6. Matt. 26:52–53.
7. Matt. 5:9.
8. James Finn, *Protest: Pacifism and Politics* (New York: Random House, 1967), p. 401.
9. James H. Forest, *Catholics and Conscientious Objection* (Catholic Peace Fellowship, 1966), p. 2.
10. "World War II." *Funk & Wagnall's New Encyclopedia.*

Chapter Two

1. Lawrence S. Wittner, *Rebels against War* (New York: Columbia University Press, 1969), p. 13.
2. Richard N. Current, T. Harry Williams, and Frank Freidel, *American History: A Survey,* 4th ed. (New York: Knopf, 1975), p. 51.
3. Ibid., p. 351.

4. John M. Blum, Bruce Catton, Edmund S. Morgan, Arthur M. Schlesinger, Jr., Kenneth M. Stampp, and C. Vann Woodward, *The National Experience,* pt. 1, 2nd ed. (New York: Harcourt, Brace & World, 1968), p. 285.
5. Diane Ravitch and Abigail Thernstrom, eds., *The Democracy Reader* (New York: HarperCollins, 1992), p. 156.
6. This famous essay is available from many sources. The quotes here are taken from Henry David Thoreau, *Walden and "Civil Disobedience"* (New York: NAL, 1980), pp. 222–240.

Chapter Three

1. Quoted in Dulaney O. Bennett, "American Friends at 75: Still for Peace and Justice," *Philadelphia Inquirer,* November 6, 1992.
2. Judith Nies, *Seven Women: Portraits from the American Radical Tradition* (New York: Viking, 1977), p. 181. The quote is by Catholic Worker member James Forest.
3. Nies, p. 138. The description was made by poet and writer Charlotte Perkins Gilman.
4. *Chronicle of the 20th Century* (Mount Kisco, New York: Chronicle, 1987), p. 217.
5. C. Roland Marchand, *The American Peace Movement and Social Reform 1898–1918* (Princeton, New Jersey: Princeton University Press, 1972), p. 266.
6. Ibid., p. 271.
7. Ibid., p. 269.
8. Marchand, p. 309.
9. Eugene V. Debs, *Walls and Bars* (Chicago: Socialist Party, 1927), p. 70.
10. Nies, p. 186.
11. Ibid., p. 188.
12. Ibid., p. 191.
13. Ibid., p. 197.
14. Finn, p. 372.
15. Ibid., p. 374.
16. Ibid., p. 375.
17. Nies, p. 200.
18. Ibid., p. 182.

Chapter Four

1. Marchand, p. 316.
2. William Allan White, *The Autobiography of William Allan White* (New York: Macmillan, 1946), p. 640.
3. Wittner, p. 11.
4. Ibid., p. 1.
5. Ibid., p. 101.
6. *History of the War Resisters League* (New York: War Resisters League, 1980), p. 4.

Chapter Five

1. Coleman McCarthy, "To Create a Peaceful World, Teach About Nonviolence," *Charlotte Observer,* October 28, 1990.
2. Webb Miller, "British India: Civil Disobedience, May 21, 1930," reprinted in *Eyewitness to History,* John Carey, ed. (New York: Avon, 1987), p. 502.
3. *News/Views,* vol. 5, no. 44, January 31, 1993, p. 5.
4. Wittner, p. 86.
5. Ibid., p. 91.
6. Kermit L. Hall, ed., *The Oxford Companion to the Supreme Court of the United States* (New York: Oxford University Press, 1992), p. 95.
7. David J. Garrow, *Bearing the Cross: Martin Luther King Jr. and the Southern Christian Leadership Conference* (New York: Morrow, 1986), pp. 11–12.
8. Ibid., p. 43.
9. *Chronicle of the 20th Century,* p. 778.
10. Ibid., p. 846.
11. Garrow, p. 75.
12. Ibid., p. 66.
13. Ibid.

Chapter Six

1. Garrow, p. 543.
2. *Chronicle of the 20th Century,* p. 941.
3. "Chronology: Generation of Conflict," *Time,* November 6, 1972, pp. 28–29.

4. *Chronicle of the 20th Century,* p. 987.
5. Writing in *Liberation,* May 1965, p. 31.
6. Ibid., 1060.
7. Phil Ochs, "The War Is Over," from the album *Tape From California.*

Chapter Seven

1. Gretchen Lemke-Santangelo, "Conscientious Objection," in *The Readers Companion to American History,* ed. Eric Foner and John A. Garraty (Boston: Houghton Mifflin, 1991), p. 215.
2. Wittner, p. 4.
3. Buffy St. Marie, "Universal Soldier," from the album *The Best of Buffy St. Marie* (Vanguard).
4. "No Tears," *Time,* February 12, 1973.
5. Allan L. Damon, "Amnesty," *American Heritage,* October 1973, p. 9.
6. David H. Hackworth, *Newsweek,* February 24, 1992.
7. Gillette v. United States, 401 U.S. 437 (1971).
8. Arlo Tatum, ed., *Handbook for Conscientious Objectors* (Philadelphia: Central Committee for Conscientious Objectors, 1966), p. 41.
9. Damon, p. 79.
10. Tatum, p. 41.
11. "Amnesty for War Resisters—ABCs of How It Will Work," *U.S. News & World Report,* September 20, 1974, p. 31.
12. Damon, p. 79.
13. Selective Service System public affairs spokesperson, interviewed, May 18, 1993.
14. Clayton Ramey of the War Resisters League, interviewed May 18, 1993.
15. *The Catholic Transcript,* November 19, 1965.

Chapter Eight

1. McCarthy, "To Create a Peaceful World."
2. Kristen Porter, "Teaching Peace," *Humanist,* May/June 1992, p. 40.
3. "The Economics of Peace," *New Yorker,* April 19, 1993.

For Further Reading

American Friends Service Committee. *Speak Truth to Power: A Quaker Search for an Alternative to Violence.* Philadelphia: American Friends Service Committee, 1944.

Axelrod, Rabbi Albert. *Call to Conscience: Jews, Judaism & Conscientious Objection.* Hoboken, New Jersey: KTAV, 1986.

Bainton, Ronald H. *Christian Attitudes toward War and Peace.* New York: Abingdon Press, 1960.

Bussey, Gertrude, and Margaret Tims. *Women's International League for Peace and Freedom 1915–1965.* London: Allen & Unwin, 1965.

Camus, Albert. *Neither Victims nor Executioners.* New York: Liberation, 1960.

Carter, Jimmy. *Talking Peace: A Vision for the Next Generation.* New York: Dutton, 1993.

Day, Dorothy. *The Long Loneliness.* New York: Harper, 1952.

Debs, Eugene V. *Walls and Bars.* Chicago: Socialist Party, 1927.

Finn, James. *Protest: Pacifism and Politics, Some Passionate Views on War and Nonviolence.* New York: Random House, 1967.

Kohn, Stephen. *Jailed for Peace: The History of American Draft Law Violators.* Westport, Conn.: Greenwood Press, 1986.

Madison, Charles A. *Critics and Crusaders: A Century of American Protest.* New York: Henry Holt, 1947.

Marchand, C. Roland. *The American Peace Movement and Social Reform 1898–1918.* Princeton, New Jersey: Princeton University Press, 1972.

Melzer, Milton. *Ain't Gonna Study War No More.* New York: Harper & Row, 1985.

Nies, Judith. *Seven Women: Portraits from the American Radical Tradition.* New York: Viking, 1977.

Wittner, Lawrence S. *Rebels against War: The American Peace Movement, 1941–1960.* New York: Columbia University Press, 1969.

Index

A
abolitionists, 42
  in Mexican war, 75
Addams, Jane, 52-56
  peace activities, 54-56, 77-78
  wins Nobel Prize, 56
African Americans, advancement, 98-99
  See also civil rights; segregation
Ali, Muhammad, 18, 137
American Alliance for Democracy, 76
American Federation of Labor (AFL), 61
American Friends Service Committee, 79
American League against War and Fascism, 77
American Peace Society, 38-39, 54
American Revolution, 37
American Union against Militarism, 55-56
Anti-Enlistment League, 136
antinuclear groups, 146
antiwar demonstrations, Chicago, 113-115
  see also Vietnam War
appeasement, rejecting, 30-31
Aquinas, St. Thomas, 25
Augustine, St., 25

B
biological warfare, 27
Black Muslims, 97
Black Panthers, 97, 114
Brethren, Church of the, 21, 37
Buddha, 21
Butler, Nicholas Murray, 56

C
capital punishment, 40
capitalism, 59
Carnegie, Andrew, 59-60
Carnegie Endowment for International Peace, 59
Catholic bishops, pastoral letter, 68
Catholic church, and pacifism, 67-69

Catholic Peace Fellowship, 145
Catholic Worker, 65-67
Catholic Worker Movement, 67, 69
Center for Teaching Peace, 83
Central Committee for Conscientious Objectors, 145
chaplains, 22
chemical warfare, 27
Chicago Seven, 114-115
China, 147
Christ, Jesus, 21
Christians, 21-22, 25, 53, 98
  pacifists, 65
Christians, early, 25
Civil Disobedience (Thoreau), 43, 46-48
civil rights movement, 92-99
  see also segregation
Civil War
  draft in, 129
  pacifists in, 74-75
class conflict, 58-59
clergy, 22
  See also Catholic church; Christians
Cleveland, President Grover, 57
Clinton, President Bill, 118
cold war, 68, 146
communism, 68
Communist Revolution, 60
Communists, in Vietnam, 104
Congress of Nations, 39
Congress of Racial Equality (CORE), 97
conscience, individual, 43-44, 45
conscientious objectors, 91-92, 131-134, 136-137, 140
  Supreme Court rulings on, 134
conscription, 38
  see also draft
Constantine I, Emperor, 21
Corwin, Senator Tom, 41
Court of Nations, 39
cowardice, 31
Crusades, 22
Czechoslovakia, 30

157